Supporting Children with Special Educational Needs

A Guide for Assistants in Schools and Pre-schools

Marian Halliwell

David Fulton Publishers
London

David Fulton Publishers Ltd

The Chiswick Centre, 414 Chiswick High Road, London W4 5TF

www.fultonpublishers.co.uk

David Fulton Publishers is a division of Granada Learning Limited, part of Granada plc.

First published 2003

10 9 8 7 6 5 4 3 2 1

Note: The right of Marian Halliwell to be identified as the author of this work has been asserted by her in accordance with the Copyright, Designs and Patents Act 1988.

Copyright © Marian Halliwell 2003

British Library Cataloguing in Publication Data
A catalogue record for this book is available from the British Library.

ISBN 1 84312 007 0

Typeset by BookEns Ltd, Royston, Herts
Printed and bound in Great Britain

Contents

Acknowledgements

This book has only been made possible by the support, encouragement and inspiration of a large number of friends and colleagues.

In particular, my thanks go to Glenys Fox, my friend and former colleague, for her invaluable advice and contributions to some of the chapters and to Elaine Atkinson for typing the manuscript.

My special thanks go to my family, Mike, Chris and Jon, who generously continue to provide my personal support system.

Marian Halliwell
Consultant for Inclusion (SEN)
School Development Service
Oxfordshire County Council
April 2003

Purpose and overview

Purpose

The purpose of this book is to enable assistants in schools and pre-schools to work more effectively in supporting children and young people who have special educational needs. It is also a book which can complement training courses.

Audience

This book is intended as a resource for:

- assistants who directly support children and young people who have special educational needs
- assistants who come into contact with children and young people who have special educational needs
- special needs coordinators and learning support coordinators in schools and pre-schools
- teachers who work in partnership with assistants to support pupils with special educational needs
- training course providers and assistants on courses.

Overview

There are sections on:

- supporting different types of special educational need
- the current context
- guidance and legislation, including the revised Code of Practice and the SEN and Disability Act
- Individual Education Plans and target setting
- working with colleagues to support learning.

Introduction

All children and young people are special. Each one has their own unique make-up and their own needs. All children benefit from additional support to help them to learn. Some need more help than others but all can and all do learn. There are some individual differences in the way children learn. Some take longer than others, some have different learning styles but all benefit from good teachers, be they the parents or carers, relatives, other children, or assistants and teachers in their schools and pre-schools. Assistants make a huge contribution in helping children to learn and this is particularly the case with children and young people who have special educational needs.

Twenty years ago, the only assistants working in mainstream schools were nursery nurses or general helpers. Special schools employed assistants to help with the care needs of pupils. Teachers and schools got by without these valuable people – it seems incredible now. The first additional assistants were appointed in the 1980s to support pupils with special educational needs in mainstream schools. This followed the 1981 Education Act, which said that 'Some pupils with special educational needs require extra help if they are to benefit from the experiences available to all pupils.' Assistants provided this 'extra help' and this is still the case today.

The number of assistants employed in schools and pre-schools continues to grow. There are now around 100,000 in England and Wales – there was a 48 per cent increase between 1995 and 2000! Assistants are known by various names; the general title of teaching assistant (TA) covers the full range. In some schools they are called learning support assistants, welfare assistants or special needs assistants. The Government has recognised the valuable contribution made by assistants and has plans to further develop their roles in supporting teaching and learning. Their contribution to the success of the literacy and numeracy strategies has already been acknowledged and, as teachers across the land can testify, they have become an indispensable part of school and pre-school life. Assistants fulfil many roles in giving support. Some work primarily with individual pupils, some with small groups, some with the whole class in partnership with the teacher. They work in a wide variety of ways and with children of all ages and abilities. Not all assistants work with children and young people who have special educational needs but many do so because this group of children tend to need additional support in order to learn effectively.

As a result of legislation and guidance to schools in 2002, many more children and young people with special educational needs are likely to attend mainstream schools. This means that, now more than ever, teachers and assistants need to be aware of the range of needs they may encounter and of the particular skills and strategies which are required to enable pupils with special needs to become successful learners, whether they are educated in special or mainstream schools.

This handbook provides a practical guide to understanding the range of special educational needs, the current context and legislation, the particular approaches which are needed to support pupils' particular needs and how you, as an assistant, can most effectively support the teachers and pupils you work with.

What are special educational needs?

Teaching assistants (TAs) play an increasingly important role in all of our schools. In particular, assistants play an essential role in supporting and raising the achievement of pupils with special educational needs. It is estimated that up to 20 per cent of all children will have special educational needs requiring additional support during their school career. Schools are becoming increasingly skilled at identifying pupils who may have special educational needs and through the use of a range of approaches are able to meet their needs and to ensure that pupils with special educational needs make progress.

> A child has special educational needs if he or she has a learning difficulty which may be the result of a physical or sensory disability, an emotional or behavioural problem, or developmental delay.
>
> (Education Act 1981)

The term special educational needs, or more usually the abbreviation SEN, is used to refer to children who find learning more difficult than the majority of children of the same age.

The children referred to as having special educational needs are very diverse. Most children develop and make good progress to reach their potential within their local mainstream schools. Many pupils need some extra help in school with subjects or activities they find difficult. Some children need some additional support and help to reach their potential. This extra support can be provided for them in a number of different ways within their mainstream schools. It may be that a pupil needs a little extra help to practise an activity or extra teaching in order to understand a new concept. For most children occasional extra help is all that is needed. Other children need more regular additional support to help them learn and make progress. Some children require additional help from SEN services or from a range of agencies that are outside the school. There are a very few children (less than 2 per cent) with SEN that are so severe or complex that the Local Education Authority (LEA) is required to assess the individual child's special educational needs and to arrange for appropriate special educational provision for that child.

In 2001 the Department for Education and Skills published a revised version of the *Special Educational Needs Code of Practice* (DfES 2001a). This document gives advice to LEAs, maintained schools and early education settings about carrying out their statutory duties. These duties include identifying, assessing and making provision for children's special educational needs.

Definition of special educational needs

Children have special educational needs if they have a learning difficulty which calls for special educational provision to be made for them.

What is a learning difficulty?

Children have a learning difficulty if they

(a) have significantly greater difficulty in learning than the majority of children of the same age; or

(b) have a disability which prevents or hinders them from making use of educational facilities of a kind generally provided for children of the same age in schools within the area of the local education authority; or

(c) are under compulsory school age and fall within the definition at (a) or (b) above or would so do if special educational provision was not made for them.

(DfES 2001a)

The definition of special educational needs in the SEN Code of Practice also specifically states that 'Children must not be regarded as having a learning difficulty solely because the language or form of language of their home is different from the language in which they will be taught.' Therefore children for whom English is an additional language must not be regarded as having special educational needs even though they may need support to help them to learn. This also means that schools and pre-school education providers need to make sure that they identify children for whom English is an additional language but who also have special educational needs.

What is special educational provision?

According to the SEN Code of Practice, special educational provision means

(a) for children of two or over, educational provision which is additional to, or otherwise different from, the educational provision made generally for children of their age in schools maintained by the LEA, other than special schools, in the area.

(b) for children under two, educational provision of any kind.

Special educational provision can be made in many ways, involving a range of different agencies from health, education or social services, and the provision usually involves a number of different professionals from a school's own staff.

All Government-funded pre-school settings must follow the SEN Code of Practice and have a written SEN policy.

The Government's Early Learning Goals (QCA 2000) set out what most children will achieve between the ages of three and five years. By the end of the Foundation Stage (the end of school Reception Year), children will have had opportunities to develop their learning in six main areas:

- personal, social and emotional development
- communication, language and literacy
- mathematical development
- knowledge and understanding of the world
- physical development
- creative development.

We know that young children in the Foundation Stage are likely to progress at different rates and some will have exceeded the Early Learning Goals. Some will have achieved the goals in some areas of learning but not in others. Some of the children making slower progress may also be learning English as an additional language. This may slow their progress in some areas but not all areas of learning and some of these children may have learning difficulties. The progress of individual children needs to be carefully monitored by schools and pre-schools so that learning opportunities can be adapted to support their learning as effectively as possible. These principles apply not only to children in the Foundation Stage (ages 3–5 years) but to all children of statutory school age (5–16 years).

The Government has also given specific guidance to schools on the teaching objectives for all pupils in Key Stages 1 and 2 in literacy and mathematics. This guidance is in the National Literacy Strategy framework (DfEE 1998a) and the National Numeracy Strategy framework (DfEE 1999b).

The trigger for special educational provision is when the rate of a child's progress in one or more areas of learning indicates that he/she may need a higher level of help than is normally provided for pupils of the same age. Schools and pre-schools should make a graduated response to the identified needs of an individual child. This means that when children have greater needs they get more support.

The SEN Code of Practice stresses that early years education settings and schools should adopt a graduated response to provide specific help to meet the child's needs through what is called Early Years Action or School Action. Early Years or School Action provides individually planned teaching and/or support which is different from or additional to what is provided for other children in the class but which enables the child to learn more effectively and to make adequate progress. Early Years or School Action may take a wide range of forms, such as giving more opportunities for a child to practise or learn skills or activities to help develop essential literacy skills. It may be in the form of additional adult supervision during activities in which the child has particular difficulty. It could be through the provision of specialist or individual equipment or resources which enable a pupil to participate in an activity more easily or successfully. Support for children with SEN is always the additional part – it is not instead of what is normally provided for all pupils.

What is the SEN Code of Practice?

The SEN Code of Practice came into effect from 1 January 2002. All LEAs, schools, early years education settings and the departments of health and social services must have regard to the Code of Practice.

The Fundamental Principles of the Code include:

- a child with special educational needs should have their needs met
- the special educational needs of children will normally be met in mainstream schools or settings
- the views of the child should be sought and taken into account
- parents have a vital role to play in supporting their child's education
- children with special educational needs should be offered full access to a broad, balanced and relevant education, including an appropriate curriculum for the Foundation Stage and the National Curriculum.

The Code of Practice gives practical guidance to LEAs, schools and the governing bodies of maintained schools in carrying out their statutory duties under the 1996 Education Act. The Code aims to ensure that

- children with SEN are identified as early as possible
- the admission of children with SEN to maintained schools in their area is monitored
- there are clear procedures for the assessment of children's SEN and for the issuing of statements

- schools are provided with support with regard to making provision for children with SEN
- provision for children with SEN is planned, audited, monitored and reviewed
- pupils with SEN are supported through School Action and School Action Plus
- training, advice and support are available for staff working with pupils with SEN
- policy and development plans are reviewed and updated regularly.

It also describes the provision for children with SEN (but not with statements) which the LEA expects to be met from maintained schools' budgets and which types of provision will be funded by the LEA.

Increasingly local education authorities have been delegating the funding for special educational needs directly to schools. This enables schools to provide flexibly for the needs of their pupils. Local education authorities are, in the main, retaining less money centrally and in most cases this is to provide support for pupils with the most severe and complex needs.

How does the SEN Code of Practice work in schools?

All pre-schools and schools must have an SEN policy. All schools and pre-school settings will have a Special Educational Needs Coordinator, usually known as the SENCO. This is a teacher or member of staff with special responsibility for ensuring the school SEN policy is put into practice. The SENCO will make sure all pupils with SEN have their needs identified and that the planning for their teaching takes account of any special educational needs pupils might have. The role of the SENCO has been changing in recent years from being the provider of direct support to a child to being a coordinator and facilitator within a school. The SENCO gathers relevant information and advice on individual pupils, advises colleagues on how to support pupils with a wide range of needs and supports and monitors the progress of these pupils. With the increasing number of teaching assistants in schools, management of TAs has become a major role for many SENCOs.

There is now an emphasis on the early identification of special educational needs. All early years education providers must appoint a SENCO and make efforts to identify any child who may have special educational needs as early as possible. The assessment of a child's needs is a continuous and ongoing process, not a single event.

How do you identify a child with special educational needs?

As an assistant you will be working regularly with small groups of children or individual children and you may have more opportunities than the class teacher to observe a child; for example, how s/he attempts activities, plays with other children, responds to instructions. You will also be well placed to notice when a child is having a particular difficulty or does not seem to be learning or progressing in the same way as the other children in a group. Often the identification of a child's special educational needs is the culmination of observations in school or pre-school, parental concern and lack of response to the usual strategies and interventions used in the school or pre-school. It is therefore very important that assistant share and discuss any concerns about a pupil that may lead to additional support through Early Years or School Action.

The indications of a child having SEN can include:

- the child has persistent emotional or behavioural problems that do not respond to the normal strategies and management techniques used in the school or pre-school setting
- the child makes little progress in spite of additional support
- the child appears to have a problem with vision or hearing that has not responded to the wearing of glasses or hearing aids
- the child has continued difficulties in communicating and/or interacting with others despite support and encouragement
- the child is working significantly below the levels expected for children of a similar age.

What is School Action?

When a child is identified as having special educational needs in a school or early years setting, the school should develop a plan to provide additional support or teaching that is different from the normal differentiated teaching that is provided for the rest of the class. This individual plan is known as an Individual Education Plan (IEP). The IEP will specify three or four short-term learning or behaviour targets for the pupil. The plan will indicate the strategies that will be used to support the achievement of the targets and the resources that will be needed. The resources may be in the form of an intervention programme, specific activities or additional human resources, which is very often a TA! Individual Education Plans will be discussed in more detail in Chapter 2. The development of an IEP for a pupil and the regular monitoring of its effectiveness by the class teacher in collaboration with parents and the SENCO is referred to as School Action.

What is School Action Plus?

Most children with special educational needs will have their needs met and will be able to make adequate progress with the additional support described in the IEP and various forms of support through School Action, but for some pupils the support provided through their IEP and School Action is not sufficient to meet their needs. The SENCO in a pre-school setting or in a school will, in consultation with colleagues, hold a meeting with the child's parents to review the child's IEP. The aim of the meeting will be to monitor the amount of progress the child has made in achieving the targets on his/her IEP.

If the child appears to have made little or no progress on the IEP targets despite receiving an individualised programme and support and there are other factors such as

- the child continues to work at a level considerably below the level expected of children of a similar age
- little or no progress has been made over a long period
- the child has emotional or behavioural difficulties which disrupt the child's learning or the learning of other children, despite having an individualised programme designed to manage the behaviour
- the child has a language or communication difficulty or a sensory or physical impairment that requires specialised equipment or resources,

the SENCO, with the agreement of the parents or carers, can request further advice from outside agencies, such as the educational psychology service or a specialist support service for hearing or visually impaired pupils. These services may carry out more detailed assessment and give advice on different strategies and resources that could be used to help support the pupil. In some cases these external agencies may visit the school or pre-school setting at regular intervals to monitor the child's progress and to update the advice on how best to support the child. In some cases advice may be sought from health service professionals, e.g. speech therapists or occupational therapists.

What is a statutory assessment?

LEAs must identify and make a statutory assessment of these children for whom they are responsible who have special educational needs and who probably need a statement.

(Education Act 1996)

A small minority of pupils, about 1–2 per cent, have difficulties which are severe and/or complex. Sometimes when a school reviews a child's progress it may be apparent that the additional programme of support provided for the child through School Action Plus is not enabling the pupil to make adequate progress. The school or parents can make a request to the LEA to carry out a statutory assessment of special educational needs. Parents can request that the LEA carries out a statutory assessment under Section 328 or 329 of the Education Act 1996. In either case the LEA must decide and tell the parents within six weeks whether or not they will make a statutory assessment.

LEAs will have a leaflet or document for parents and schools about their policy and the procedure for requesting a statutory assessment for a child. The LEA will gather together all the relevant information and evidence about the child and his/her needs. This will include information on what support the child has received through School Action Plus, what progress the child has made and whether advice has been received from an educational psychologist, or from a specialist teacher, or whether medical advice has been sought. The views of the parents and any other professionals involved with the child will be sought and the views of the child should also be included. When the evidence has been gathered the LEA will make a decision as to whether to carry out a statutory assessment which could lead to a statement of special educational needs for the child. If the LEA decides to carry out a statutory assessment, there is a legal requirement for the process to be completed within 26 weeks and the parents must be informed in writing of the LEA's intention to carry out a statutory assessment.

Parent Partnership Services now exist in all authorities to give parents of children with special educational needs support and advice through trained volunteers known as independent parent advisers. Parents will be asked to contribute to the assessment and the social services department and health authority will be informed that the LEA is proposing to carry out an assessment of a child and will be asked for relevant information on the child.

If the LEA decides not to make a statutory assessment they must explain their reasons in writing to the parents and set out the provision that they consider would meet the child's needs. If the LEA decides to carry out an assessment they must make sure that the process is completed within 26 weeks. The LEA must seek advice from parents, the school educational psychologist, health professionals, social services and any other appropriate source. The revised Code places more emphasis on the views of the child also having to be sought as a contribution to the information being gathered about themselves. Having received all the advice the LEA must decide whether it needs to write a statement.

If the LEA decides that the child's special educational needs can be met from the school's own resources through School Action or School Action Plus and therefore a statement is not necessary, the LEA must write to the parents giving their reasons and tell parents of their right to appeal to the SEN and Disability Tribunal against the decision. When an LEA decides to issue a statement they must give parents a copy of the proposed statement. The statement will describe in detail the provision considered necessary to meet the child's special educational needs and it must be written in the form prescribed in the SEN Regulations (DfES 2001a). The statement will also name the school where the child's needs can be met. The parents or carers will receive a written copy of the statement and have 15 days in which to discuss the proposed statement with the LEA if they disagree with any element of it. After 15 days the LEA will send the parents a final statement. Parents have a right of appeal to the SEN and Disability Tribunal if they disagree with the provision specified in the statement.

The progress of a child who has a statement of special educational needs will usually be monitored through reviewing IEPs at least twice a year but the statement must be reviewed at least once each year at the Annual Review.

What is the Disability Discrimination Act?

In September 2002 the Special Educational Needs and Disability Act 2001 (SENDA) came into force making it unlawful for any school to discriminate against disabled pupils with regard to admissions, exclusions or access to educational and associated services. The term 'discrimination' means to treat disabled pupils less favourably than pupils who are not disabled. A Code of Practice has been produced as guidance for schools.

The Disability Discrimination Act 1995 (DDA) defines a disabled person as someone who has a physical or mental impairment which has a substantial and long-term adverse effect on his or her ability to carry out normal day-to-day activities. This is a broad definition and includes pupils with physical, sensory, intellectual or mental impairments. Pupils with a learning disability, sensory impairment, severe diabetes, epilepsy or dyslexia, severe disfigurement or a progressive condition may be included. The Disability Discrimination Act complements the SEN framework.

Many children with SEN will be defined as disabled under the definition of the Disability Discrimination Act, but not all children who are defined as disabled will have special educational needs; for example, a pupil with severe diabetes or asthma.

All pre-school and school settings are obliged to ensure that they avoid discrimination against disabled pupils in all aspects of school life, admissions, exclusions. The reference to education and associated services includes not only teaching and learning opportunities but the whole range of extra-curricular activities including school trips, school clubs, and lunchtime activities.

Schools have two key responsibilities:

- not to treat disabled pupils less favourably
- to make reasonable adjustment for disabled pupils.

If a school is unable to make reasonable adjustment for disabled pupils, the school must have evidence that there is a substantial reason why the adjustment cannot be made. Factors such as cost, health and safety issues and the interests of other pupils are taken into account when considering what reasonable adjustment a school should make. Parents have a right of appeal to the SEN and Disability Tribunal if they feel that their disabled child has been discriminated against and a school has not made reasonable adjustment.

Teaching assistants play a vital role in ensuring that disabled pupils are included in our schools. Very often schools will include support from a TA for a disabled pupil as part of the 'reasonable adjustment' that the school makes to meet the pupil's needs.

TAs take on a variety of roles to support disabled students in the wide range of day-to-day school activities. This may include support with personal or self-help needs, differentiating curriculum materials, planning and developing with teachers practical strategies and resources that will support a pupil.

2 Target setting and Individual Education Plans

We know that children develop and learn new skills and behaviours progressively and that in many cases learning needs to take place in a particular sequence in order for a child to develop or master more complex concepts, skills and behaviours. For children with special educational needs or disabilities the rate of progress in their development may be much slower or their ability to acquire and develop skills, in particular areas of learning, may be impaired or limited by the nature of their special educational needs and/or disabilities. Progress is often made in very small steps.

Guidance on targets for pupils with special educational needs

To help teachers and Early Years practitioners ensure that they plan and provide an effective curriculum that enables all children to make the best possible progress, national guidance has been provided. For Early Years (children aged three to five years) there is the *Curriculum Guidance for the Foundation Stage* (QCA 2000). It gives guidance to help with the planning and teaching in six areas of learning:

- personal, social and emotional development
- communication, language and literacy
- mathematical development
- knowledge and understanding of the world
- physical development
- creative development.

The Guidance contains 'Stepping Stones' which are descriptions of what a child needs to learn in order to achieve the Early Learning Goals by the end of the Foundation Stage (the end of Reception Year).

For older pupils the DfES has issued guidance for teachers on the effective planning and teaching of literacy and mathematics in the form of the National Literacy Strategy for Key Stages 1, 2 and 3 and the National Numeracy Strategy for Key Stages 1, 2 and 3, (DfEE 1998a, DfEE 1999b) as well as the National Curriculum guidance for all the individual subjects taught in schools. The progress and performance of pupils and schools is monitored through the Standard Assessment Tasks, better known as SATs, which are set for pupils at the end of each Key Stage in Years 2, 6 and 9 for English, maths and science (known as the core subjects)

Many pupils with special educational needs will not be achieving at the same level as their peers. For pupils who are working at a level below National Curriculum Level 1, there is guidance for schools giving details of suitable finely graded learning objectives (DfES 2001c, 2002). These documents give detailed descriptions and examples of what pupils should be able to do at each of the eight progressive P levels which lead to Level 1 of the National Curriculum in mathematics and English respectively. For pupils functioning at the lowest levels, P1 to P3, the performance descriptions are common for all subjects. They describe a gradual increase in awareness of the environment and responses to interactions, objects and people indicating the early development of non-verbal and verbal communication skills.

Many pupils with special educational needs will be working at levels significantly below the level expected for their chronological age. Their rate of progress will also be slower and the development of their skills is likely to progress in more finely graded stages. In monitoring the progress of all pupils, teachers will identify where there may be a widening gap between a pupil and the attainment of his peers.

Teachers should then track back in the learning objectives provided in the National Literacy and Numeracy Strategy teaching frameworks (DfEE 1998a, DfEE 1999b). This means looking back in the teaching framework to earlier learning objectives until objectives are reached where the pupil's learning is secure. The learning objectives from the teaching frameworks or the P level descriptions can then form the basis for the planning to move the pupil forward in his/her learning to the next objective.

Having tracked back to where the pupil's learning is secure, most skilled teachers can usually meet the needs of pupils with SEN through flexible teaching, good differentiation of teaching strategies and learning outcomes. Where a pupil's progress is giving cause for concern, the teacher will try to help the child by making further adjustments to how the child is taught. This may involve adjusting the pace of teaching and changing the strategies used to support the child. Often support may also be given by placing the child in a different or smaller teaching group where additional support can be provided. In many cases, additional support will be a teaching assistant working with an individual or group of pupils.

What are effective targets?

Effective targets are learning targets which are derived from the careful assessment of an individual pupil's needs. These targets identify the next stage of learning that needs to be achieved in order for the pupil to progress towards longer-term learning targets. We know that children with SEN often only make slow progress, in very finely graded steps. The targets on an Individual Education Plan (IEP) give details of what should be taught next.

Targets are generally most effective when they are 'SMART'; that is, they are

Specific
Measurable
Achievable
Relevant
Time limited.

Specific means that the learning target is clear and precise and is not too general.

Measurable means that a judgement can be made as to whether the target has been achieved or not. IEP targets should also give details of how well something has to be learned before it is considered to be mastered.

Achievable means that the target is realistic and can be achieved in a relatively short time.

Relevant means that the target is relevant to the pupil's needs and leads to longer-term goals or is the next stage in development of key areas in communication, behaviour, literacy or mathematics.

Time limited means that the target is planned to be achievable for the pupil within a relatively short period of time, i.e. weeks rather than months. Targets that take too long to achieve can lead to the pupil losing motivation and giving up!

'Targets that take too long to achieve can lead to the pupil losing motivation and giving up'

Targets on IEPs will not be effective if they are too challenging and cannot be achieved within a reasonable time, but care also needs to be taken that targets are not too easy to achieve. The best and most effective targets are those that are attainable with some additional support and which enable the pupil to feel s/he is making real progress.

Why do we need targets?

Targets are important for all of us in our daily lives. We set ourselves targets every day though we are not always aware of it – to finish the ironing, for instance, or to get the shopping on the way home. In school, teachers, support staff and pupils all have targets to achieve on a daily basis. Teachers plan how to deliver the curriculum at whole-school level, for particular year groups or classes, for groups within classes and for individual pupils.

Planning and setting targets is a very important element of effective teaching that ensures that all pupils receive their educational entitlement. By setting targets we are clear about what needs to be taught, how it can be taught and then we can assess whether the teaching has been successful in enabling pupils to make progress.

Setting individual targets and planning individually for pupils enables schools to monitor the progress of all pupils including pupils who may have a range of severe and/or complex needs. It ensures that all pupils are progressing even if progress is much slower and in much more finely graded steps than that of the majority of pupils in the school.

What is an IEP?

When pupils have special educational needs the planning and target setting has to be individually tailored to a pupil's needs to ensure that every pupil makes maximum progress. Individual Education Plans are part of a clear system within schools to ensure that the needs of all pupils are identified and assessed and that effective teaching and appropriate support is planned and delivered to enable pupils to make progress.

An IEP is a detailed planning document which relates to the learning needs of an individual pupil on the SEN register who may be either at School Action or School Action Plus or have a statement of special educational needs.

The aim of the IEP is to identify three or four clear individual learning targets which when attained by the pupil will enable him/her to progress and where possible catch up with his/her peers. An IEP specifies a pupil's learning targets and the planning and teaching for that pupil which will be different from that of the rest of the class. In practical terms an IEP is a record of the progressive learning targets. It details how the pupil will be supported, what strategies will be used, who will provide the additional support and when that support will be provided.

What are success criteria?

Good IEPs will also indicate the success criteria for achieving the target. How will the pupil, teachers and support staff know when a target has been achieved? In many cases success criteria will not only detail what has to be achieved, but the level of accuracy or frequency that has to be achieved; e.g.,

if the target on an IEP is
I will learn to spell the following words by the end of term: they, where, many, who, other,
the success criteria may be
I will write each word with 80 per cent accuracy in my independent writing.

The teaching strategies to enable this to be achieved may be

- To practise the target words twice each day in school and once at home using: Look, read, spell, cover, write, check strategy
- Daily practice using Starspell ICT program and board/card games to support over-learning
- To proofread independent writing to highlight target words and check for accuracy
- Assistant to support proofreading of written work and daily practice sessions
- Parents to support at home.

IEPs should be reviewed at least twice a year. In many schools IEPs are reviewed termly and in some cases more frequently. Progress should be monitored and targets adjusted or new targets set. IEPs can be written in different formats. Often school and/or LEAs have a standard proforma for IEPs which helps to ensure that the IEPs contain all the necessary information and are easy to access by a range of staff. In all cases IEPs should include the following information:

- short-term targets set for or by the pupil
- the teaching strategies to be used
- the provision to be put in place
- when the plan is to be reviewed
- success/exit criteria
- outcomes (to be recorded when IEP is reviewed).

(DfES 2001b: Section 5)

IEPs are intended to be working documents that should be used in the classroom, not pieces of paper that are stored in folders in filing cabinets. It is expected that they will be altered and annotated between the reviews of each IEP to reflect the achievements of the pupil.

The role of the assistant in supporting effective IEPs

Teaching assistants are often closely involved with the planning, delivery and monitoring of IEPs for individual pupils and sometimes for groups of pupils.

As a TA it is essential that you have easy access to the IEPs of children whom you support. Assistants and the pupils need to know and understand what the targets are and how they will be achieved. Very often assistants will be involved in delivering and supervising the planned intervention which will enable the pupil to achieve the targets.

The implementation of the IEP is the responsibility of the class or subject teacher, often in collaboration with the SENCO. In practice TAs, under the supervision of a teacher, will often be responsible for the direct support of pupils in lessons and, in many cases, the delivery of differentiated support. It is essential that assistants should be clear about what the targets are for each pupil and also be trained in differentiating the support that each pupil will require. They need to be confident in using a range of strategies and familiar with a variety of resources that are to be used to support the pupil's learning.

TAs will need training in order to be confident in delivering a programme of intervention or in using particular resources. Training comes in many different forms and does not always necessitate attending a formal training course. Some of the most effective training occurs when a teacher or more experienced TA models or demonstrates how to deliver an intervention programme or how to use a specific resource with the pupils. You need to remember that teachers will usually be on hand to advise and support assistants in working with pupils.

IEPs are usually reviewed at least termly and must be reviewed at least twice a year. If an assistant has been involved in delivering and supporting an IEP, it is important that he/she is consulted as part of the review process. Invariably assistants can provide vital information about the progress a pupil has made in achieving targets by keeping written records, but often they are able to give insights into the pupil's motivation, self-esteem and particular strengths or weaknesses if they can take part in the review discussion.

Assistants can also provide invaluable contributions to the discussion leading to the review and setting of new targets. Participating in the discussion

Don't aim too high — or too low!

and planning of new IEPs enables TAs to understand not only the targets but also the thinking and reasoning behind the setting of specific targets. It also provides opportunities to discuss with teaching staff, parents and other professionals the most effective ways of differentiating the work and supporting a pupil. The review of an IEP provides an opportunity for all those involved including the pupil, to review the progress made and to work together to set the most appropriate targets and plan the most effective support strategies.

How do we measure progress on IEPs?

Measuring progress and deciding when a pupil has achieved a target on their IEP is not always as easy as it seems. Do we say a pupil has achieved a target if they have achieved it on one occasion? Anyone who has worked with children with special educational needs knows that, like all of us, they have good days and not so good days. Therefore we have to be clear as to when a target has been achieved.

This leads us to the concept of mastery. How well do you have to be able to do something in order to say you have really learned it and retain that ability to do it over time? It is not always easy to be absolutely specific, but when an IEP is written it should state not only the learning target but also the criteria that need to be met in order to say that the pupil has really achieved the target. For example,

if the target on an IEP is
I will learn to spell the words – have, many, they, there, more
how will we decide when each of these words has been learned? If you give the pupil a spelling test and ask him/her to write the words down, will that really test whether they have mastered the spelling of each of these words? We have to ask, 'What is it we really want the pupil to be able to do?' Is being able to spell the words in isolation in a specific test sufficient? Or do we want the pupil to be able to use and spell the words correctly in their independent writing without the need for support? An IEP needs to state clearly not only what the learning target is, but also how we will know that it has been achieved.
The IEP needs to state the target:
I will learn the words – have, many, they, there, more,
and also the criteria for achievement:
I will be able to use and write the words correctly in my independent writing without the need for support.
In some cases it may also be good practice to state specifically what level of accuracy is required before a target is achieved:
The success criteria will be spelling the words at least 80 per cent correct in independent writing.

Measuring progress is not always easy when the area of difficulty is behaviour. In developing an IEP, careful thought needs to be given not only to the target but also to how progress will be recognised and measured. We often want children to stop negative behaviour as a target. For example, we may want a pupil to stop shouting out during the oral and mental starter in the daily mathematics lesson. Therefore the IEP target may focus on reducing the unwanted behaviour and using a more appropriate behaviour: *I will stop shouting out in the oral and mental starter in the daily maths lesson and will put up my hand when I want to say something.*

In order to measure progress on this target we will need to know how often the shouting out was occurring in the oral and mental starter of the maths lesson before the intervention was started. We will need to monitor and record whether the frequency of shouting out reduces with the introduction of an intervention strategy.

TAs are often asked to observe and to record behavioural occurrences in order to measure progress on behavioural targets.

For the behavioural target:
I will stop shouting out in the oral and mental starter in the daily maths lesson and I will put up my hand when I want to say something,
regular monitoring of the number of times the pupil shouts out and/or puts his hand up must be kept – this could be done as a bar chart or graph so that the pupil can see whether he or she is making progress. When the IEP is planned, the criteria for successfully achieving the target need to be clear. Will the target be achieved if the pupil does not shout out in one lesson? Clear criteria for achieving that target would be
No more than one shouting out incident per mathematics lesson over a two-week period.

Good IEPs need to consider not only the targets and intervention strategies but also how progress will be measured. Care needs to be taken to specify the context or circumstances in which the target has to be achieved. The learning targets set in IEPs need to be generalised; that is, the pupil can use that learning appropriately in a range of situations – this applies to both learning and behaviour targets. It also means that achievement criteria may need to be changed from very specific to more general application when the IEP is reviewed.

What do we mean by adequate progress?

The concept of adequate progress is not easy to define and for different pupils it will mean different things. It implies looking at targets over time to ensure that targets have been achieved and also maintained and generalised; that is, a pupil can use and adapt their learning to a variety of situations. Adequate progress is defined in the *SEN Toolkit* Section 5 (DfES 2001b) as progress which

- closes the attainment gap between the pupil and the pupil's peers
- prevents the attainment gap growing wider
- is similar to that of peers starting from the same attainment baseline, but less than that of the majority of peers
- matches or betters the pupil's previous rate of progress

- ensures access to the full curriculum
- demonstrates improvements in the pupil's behaviour
- is likely to lead to appropriate accreditation
- is likely to lead to participation in further education, training and/or employment.

What are Group Education Plans?

There may be circumstances where several children within a class or subject set have similar significant difficulties and therefore similar IEP targets. This seems to occur most commonly in mainstream classes in literacy and numeracy. In some cases it may be appropriate to use common strategies which are additional to, or different from, good differentiated teaching. This may take the form of a short daily intervention for a small withdrawal group of pupils. In such cases the pupils' common targets and strategies can be recorded in a Group Learning Plan or Group Education Plan. If pupils have additional individual targets these will need to be recorded on a separate IEP, so a Group Education Plan may be attached to an IEP where this is appropriate.

3 The role of the assistant in supporting children and young people with special educational needs

Your needs

As an assistant whose job it is to work with children and young people who have special educational needs, you will have a range of needs yourself!

- knowledge of the special educational need or needs of the child whom you are supporting and the learning implications for the child
- knowledge of the strategies which are likely to be the most effective in helping the child
- access to a teacher or another assistant who can give you guidance and answer any questions
- an awareness of your role in
  - supporting the child or young person
  - supporting the teacher
  - supporting the curriculum
  - supporting the school.

How can I support the child or young person with special educational needs?

A report produced by the Centre for Educational Needs, University of Manchester, (DfEE 1999a) defined the role by saying that effective practice

- fosters the participation of pupils in the social and academic processes of a school (or pre-school)
- seeks to enable pupils to become more independent learners
- helps to raise standards of achievement for all pupils.

Fostering participation

This means enabling and encouraging the child to join in with social and academic activities as much as possible and encouraging other children to include the child in school life. It is frequently the case that pupils with special educational needs are aware of their difficulties and this is especially the case as they get older. Your role is crucial in encouraging children to work and play together and to respect and understand differences. Some children can become bullied if they are perceived as being different in some way and many parents express fears about this happening to their child if they were to transfer from a special to a mainstream school. This depends a great deal on the culture of the school and whether differences are celebrated and valued or not.

Enabling pupils to become more independent learners

This means that pupils become confident and are able to learn without adult support. It is a very common fault of assistants that they give too much support and do not allow the pupil enough space or time to attempt their work unaided. You need to remember that one of the most effective ways to learn is through making mistakes!

Raising standards of achievement

The government is very keen to improve the test results of all pupils and this includes those with special educational needs. This means that all teachers need to be effective teachers and all assistants need to become as effective as possible in supporting the learning of pupils.

What do we mean by inclusion?

The concept of inclusion is a key part of the philosophy which underpins the guidance to schools from the Department for Education and Skills. The revised Code of Practice (DfES 2001a) is clear about this: 'the special educational needs of children will normally be met in mainstream schools or settings.'

Prior to this, in 1998, the DfEE published the Action Programme for SEN (DfEE 1998b) which had this to say about inclusion:

> Promoting inclusion within mainstream schools where parents want it and appropriate support can be provided, will remain the cornerstone of our strategy. There are strong educational, as well as social and moral grounds for educating children with SEN, or with disabilities, with their peers. This is an important part of building an inclusive society.

The National Curriculum Inclusion Statement emphasises the importance of providing effective learning opportunities for all pupils and offers the following three key principles for inclusion:

- setting suitable learning challenges
- responding to pupils' diverse needs
- overcoming potential barriers to learning and assessment for individuals and groups of pupils.

We all need to belong, to be included in social and family groups. It is a basic human need, second in rank only to the survival needs of warmth, food and shelter. If you think back, you can probably remember a time when you felt included and part of a group you really wanted to be with. Perhaps you were picked for a team event or invited to a particular social occasion. You may also be able to recall, as most people can, times when you were not included in an event which you really wanted to be part of, perhaps this was a social group, a team or a family situation. As you consider these past experiences you will probably be able to remember the *feelings* associated with times you were included and the times you felt excluded

Feelings associated with	
Inclusion	**Exclusion**
• Accepted	• Rejected
• Valued	• Upset
• At ease	• Angry
• Content	• Frustrated
• Happy	• Hard done by
• Useful	• Unhappy
	• Useless

The words associated with exclusion are commonly used in the vocabulary of a considerable number of adults in our society who have a disability or a learning difficulty, some of whom were educated in special schools. They express feelings of being cut off to some extent, either because of access difficulties, such as to public transport or public buildings, or because of other people's attitudes. There is still considerable ignorance about disability which the Government is seeking to change both through legislation (the Special Educational Needs and Disability Act 2001) and through policy. It is recognised that there will be a continuing role for special schools in the immediate future but that their role will be different from in the past, as they increase their links with mainstream schools. Inclusive education means that children with special educational needs can learn together with other children from their neighbourhoods in their local schools and pre-schools. There are three key factors which underpin inclusion, and all three need to be right for inclusion to be successful. Assistants have an important part to play in making this happen.

Three key factors:

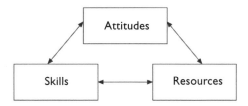

Attitudes

First and foremost pre-school and school staff must have the right attitudes. They must be ready and willing to accept all children and the school policies must reflect this whole-school approach. The attitudes of all adults who work in schools need to be such that they are working to encourage the participation of all children in both the academic and the social life of the school. The attitudes of assistants are important. They need to be aware that children have more similarities than differences and they need to work to include children with special educational needs in the main activities of the class wherever possible.

Skills

Assistants sometimes feel rather daunted at the prospect of supporting pupils with special educational needs, particularly if the child has complex needs. Some may feel that they do not yet have the necessary skills to give the right support. However, much can be learned through training, reading or observation – watching good teachers working with pupils enables you to see which approaches best meet particular needs.

Resources

Assistants may need to learn how particular resources help particular children. This is increasingly the case in respect of computer-aided learning programmes, which can be very helpful to pupils developing literacy and numeracy skills. There are a number of packages with lesson guidelines developed by the literacy and numeracy strategies which assistants or teachers can use in helping pupils to improve their literacy and numeracy skills. Some children will need help with specific equipment such as hearing aids or callipers. There will be teachers in the school or specialist teachers available to guide assistants in giving this support. And, of course, assistants themselves are probably the most important resource in making inclusion work in the classroom through their work in encouraging and enabling the pupil to be accepted, happy and settled.

It will help if you remember these three ideas:

- Children have more similarities than differences
- Everyone has a range of needs
- Support is available to enable you to do your job.

There is, however, one big trap which awaits you in your support role – a trap which does not support inclusion – and these extracts contain examples of this, taken from some work about inclusion where the writer observed what was going on in one classroom:

> A current area of practice that seems to lead to feelings of exclusion concerns the role of classroom assistants .... I looked closely at the impact of their work in pupil participation in one secondary school. In art, for example, two pupils (with special educational needs) completed the tasks of the lesson, even though they were both absent! In fact, the classroom assistant did the work for them.
>
> In general, our impression was that, whilst the pupils seen as having special needs were following broadly the same activities as their classmates, the constant presence of a 'helper' meant that often the challenges posed by these activities were significantly reduced.
>
> (Ainscow 1998)

It is very easy to fall into the trap of doing too much for the pupil, which encourages their dependence on you and reduces their confidence in working independently.

Your role is *not* to do the task for the pupil

What factors influence learning?

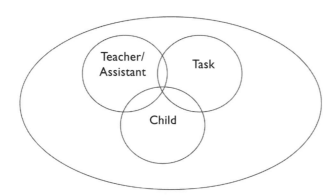

This diagram shows the factors which work together to influence learning. Teaching assistants need to be aware of these interlinking factors:

- The task should be at the right level – the child should be able to understand it.
- The adult working with the child – teacher or assistant – should work with the child at the right level and pace, showing sensitivity to their needs.
- The child's abilities, motivation, physical and emotional well-being can vary and influence how they learn.
- The environment needs to be right (for example, the classroom may need to be quiet or noisy; the child may be better working next to a child who is a good role model or in a smaller group).

Special educational needs used to be seen as a problem within the child. Over the last 20 years it has been seen as a relative term, dependent to an extent on the learning environment and the task to be done. So, in your role as an assistant you will need to remember that, when learning difficulties occur, it may be something to do with the task being too hard or not being explained well enough. 'If tasks and activities in which the learner is engaged are not matched to the learner's capabilities, or are not understood by the learner, then learning difficulties are likely to occur' (Ainscow and Tweddle 1988).

This shows us the importance of getting the learning activity right – you would not, for example, give a three-year-old a page of maths to do! It also shows us that the adult working with the child must be sensitive to providing activities which are achievable by the child. This is the case for *all* children, not just those who benefit from additional support. Presenting a child with a task which is too hard leads them to feel unsuccessful, and this sometimes puts them off learning. It is not just the task but also the way it is presented and the learning environment which influence the confidence and the abilities of the learners. Your job is to help in creating conditions for the child to learn as well as they can.

Overcoming barriers to learning

Have you ever tried to learn a new skill and found it harder than you thought? Imagine that you are sitting in a car and have to drive from London to Paris. You have a map and a full tank of petrol. Think of all the skills and abilities you need to do this task:

- Map reading
- Good eyesight
- Mobility in arms and legs
- Knowledge of how to drive the car
- Confidence
- Handling money – English and French
- Knowledge of where to buy the ticket to cross the Channel.

What might be the barriers to learning how to do this and how might they be overcome?

Barriers (what's stopping you)	How to overcome them
• Can't read maps	➢ Get someone to help / write directions
• Poor eyesight / visual impairment	➢ Get a chauffeur
• Use of only one arm	➢ Get a chauffeur
• Use of only one leg	➢ Use an automatic car
• Cannot drive the car	➢ Take lessons
• Lacking in confidence	➢ Try a shorter trip first / take a friend
• Cannot handle money	➢ Use a credit card
• Don't know where to buy the ticket	➢ Contact travel agent and pre-arrange

What can we learn from this?

- The first thing we notice is that all people are different – they are at different stages of development, they start the task with different skills and need different forms of help to be successful; for instance, some might need help with map reading, others with handling foreign currency.

- Confidence is very necessary.
- Correct strategies are necessary.
- Other people can help (or hinder if they make us feel worse).
- Learners become motivated if they are successful or anxious if they are not.
- The teaching method is all-important – the teacher has to have the correct knowledge and be encouraging.
- We continue to build on our learning and get better at tasks until we have mastered them.

Most pupils are expected to develop their knowledge, understanding and skills every day. Learning seems to come naturally to some children but most find certain subjects or concepts difficult at some point in their school lives. For pupils with special educational needs there can be enormous barriers to their learning. Lack of confidence can be a real problem. It is hard for young people, particularly in the teenage years, to see others being able to do what they find difficult and so frequently they give up – what is the point? Many pupils who have special educational needs have difficulty in learning to read and write and yet the curriculum includes many lessons where these skills are necessary for success. It is therefore very important to start with what the pupil *can* do and work towards the next step. Presenting activities which are too hard puts children off learning and, when this happens day after day, it is little wonder that they switch off.

As an assistant giving support, your main task will be to judge what activity is right for the pupil in order to learn effectively. It is all too easy to do the task for them or to jump in before you should. Pupils need time to think and encouragement to try new things.

The assistant's role

Supporting the teacher

Different teachers will want different things from you and, to some extent, what you *can* do is constrained or encouraged by the teachers' understanding and expectations of your role. Teachers have identified the following tasks for assistants in supporting pupils with special educational needs:

- Working together
- Assessing, reporting and recording progress
- Help in setting targets
- Providing feedback
- Delivering specialist programmes
- Managing specialist equipment
- Supporting personal needs.

Working together

It is essential that the teacher makes clear to you what is needed in the lesson so your time is used efficiently and effectively. Good teachers will be sharing their lesson plans with you so you are clear about your responsibilities. The Audit Commission report of 1992 made this clear: 'If a small amount of the time currently spent alongside pupils were re-directed into planning and discussion about individual pupils between support and classroom teachers, there would be a significant improvement in effectiveness.'

Assessing and reporting progress

Assistants have many qualities but this is an area which many assistants find difficult. It will help the teacher a good deal if you are able to make an accurate assessment of what the pupil has learned during the lesson and, equally important, what they have *not* learned. This sort of assessment is called formative assessment because it informs and tells us more about what the next step is for the pupil. It is not uncommon to find descriptive accounts, in the records kept by assistants, of the tasks done by the pupil in the lesson. However, it is not as common to find the useful section which should follow; that is, an evaluation of what the pupil can and can't do followed by a recommendation of what, therefore, should be covered in the next lesson.

Target setting

If assessment is done well enough, then target setting becomes easy. As an assistant you may be involved in setting targets for the specific lessons ('By the end of this lesson, I expect Jason to be able to . . .'). If you are able to do this, remember to involve the pupil in the process if at all possible and do remember to keep the target realistic and achievable – or else the pupil will become very dispirited and lose motivation.

Providing feedback

As well as providing feedback about what the pupil has learned and giving your views on the 'what next?' issues, you have a key role in feeding back to the teacher anything else you may pick up about the pupil. So you may recognise that he or she is upset, tired or angry or that he or she has come to school without breakfast or that the dog has died – there are many things in the lives of children and young people which affect their abilities to settle and learn in the classroom and assistants are often the people who pick up on these things and are then able to inform the teacher.

Delivering specialist programmes

Pupils with special educational needs often require special arrangements to help them and assistants are frequently called upon by teachers to deliver these programmes. Children with language difficulties may require some daily practice to develop speaking and listening skills. Speech and language therapists often devise programmes for assistants to work on with pupils. In the case of physical disabilities, the physiotherapist or the occupational therapist is likely to request that you work with the child on particular exercises and movement sequences. For pupils with literacy or numeracy difficulties, there are a number of specialist schemes of work which you may be called upon to deliver. Always make sure you are clear about what is required and do ask questions if you are unsure.

Managing specialist equipment

Some children and young people require specialist equipment; for instance, pupils with cerebral palsy require callipers or splints. Your role may entail adjusting these aids and making sure the child is comfortable. If you support pupils with hearing impairment you may need to be trained in the use of hearing aids so that they are comfortable and work efficiently.

Supporting personal needs

The teacher may ask you to assist the child in feeding or in using the toilet. In these situations you need to be particularly sensitive to the feelings of the child or young person and to allow them to be as independent as possible.

Supporting the curriculum

More and more assistants are being asked to give support to enable the pupil to 'access the curriculum'.

Guidance from the Department for Education and Skills (2001a) states:

The curriculum in all schools should be balanced, broadly based and aim to:

- provide opportunities for all pupils to learn and achieve
- promote pupils' spiritual, moral, social and cultural development and prepare all pupils for the opportunities, responsibilities and experiences of life.

These two aims are independent and reinforce each other. The personal development of pupils plays a significant part in their ability to learn and achieve.

and

For pupils with learning difficulties the school curriculum might aim to:

- enable pupils to interact and communicate with a wide range of people
- enable pupils to express preferences, communicate needs, make choices, make decisions and choose options that other people act on and respect
- promote self-advocacy or the use of a range of systems of supported advocacy
- prepare pupils for an adult life in which they have the greatest possible degree of autonomy and support them in having relationships with mutual respect and dependence on each other
- increase pupils' awareness and understanding of their environment and of the world
- encourage pupils to explore, to question and to challenge
- provide a wide range of learning experiences for pupils in each key stage suitable for their age.

and, about the role of support staff,

All support staff can add to, and support the curriculum so long as joint working practices help the exchange of information and the discussion of learning opportunities and provide ways to review pupils' progress.

The National Curriculum has several key stages:

The Foundation Stage	3–5 years	(pre-schools and Year R)
Key Stage 1	5–7 years	(Years 1 and 2)
Key Stage 2	7–11 years	(Years 3, 4, 5, 6)
Key Stage 3	11–14 years	(Years 7, 8, 9)
Key Stage 4	14–16 years	(Years 10 and 11)
Post-16	16–18 years	(Years 12 and 13)

Each key stage has levels of attainment in each subject which pupils are expected to achieve, starting at Level 1. However, pupils who have learning difficulties are often slower to progress through the levels than other children of the same age. Some have such significant learning difficulties that they never achieve Level 1 and are said to be working towards that level. This pre-Level 1 stage has been divided into smaller steps which are known as 'P levels'. You need to know about these levels if you are working with pupils who have severe and/or complex needs.

If you work in a primary or secondary school you will become familiar with what most pupils are able to achieve at each key stage. For pupils with special educational needs, your job will be to know what is expected of the child and to remove the barriers to learning discussed earlier in this chapter. You may well have to become knowledgeable yourself about a range of subjects, especially in secondary schools, where it is becoming more common for assistants to be attached to curriculum areas.

Supporting the school

There are a range of ways in which you will be able to give support to the school:

- teamwork with teachers
- supporting whole-school events
- attending whole-school training (as relevant)
- knowing the school routines and procedures.

In supporting pupils with special educational needs your main contribution to the school's responsibilities will be contributing to reviews of the pupils' progress and communicating with parents.

Contributing to reviews

All pupils who are supported through School Action or Action Plus should be reviewed regularly to assess their progress and set new targets. Pupils with statements have a statutory Annual Review (see Chapter 2). If you know the child well, you may be asked to attend the meeting and give a short verbal or written report about their progress and their needs. The teachers you work with will help you to prepare for these review meetings as they will need to be clear about your contributions. Occasionally there may be case conferences about the pupils you support. Sometimes these follow an exclusion from school or a concern about child protection issues. Social services or health services are often involved. It is important that you give your views in line with the school's views about the child's needs. You will be able to discuss your contribution *before* these important meetings. You will need the skills of sensitivity and clarity on these occasions.

Working with parents or carers

If the pupil has significant difficulties and requires a lot of personal care from you, then you may be in contact with the parents or carers quite frequently, and in doing this you are representing the school. If home–school links are difficult, you may need to encourage these links to be more positive. It is sometimes quite hard for parents to accept that their child has a problem and expectations can sometimes be too high, or indeed too low if parents see their child as unable to achieve much. You will need to work to enable realistic expectations to be set and it will be really helpful if you can inform parents about the progress of pupils. Sometimes pupils with complex needs demand a lot of time and attention from parents and may indeed need it if their personal needs are significant. You will need to recognise the pressures on these parents and be prepared to lend a 'listening ear' as appropriate. But do remember to keep a safe emotional distance and do not get drawn into difficult family situations. Keep the teachers informed if you have concerns.

4 Working with other professionals

Supporting and meeting the needs of all the pupils with special educational needs in a school is not only very important, it is often a very complex task. It will involve all the staff of the school – head teacher, SENCO, class teachers, assistants and administrative staff – in a variety of different roles. For pupils at School Action Plus and those with statements, a range of professionals from the LEA support services and also from the health service or social services may be involved.

Assistants may need to work with a range of professionals at different times. It is important that assistants have a job description and clear understanding of their own role and the lines of communication within a school.

What is the role of a TA in school?

TAs provide support in a number of different ways that fall into four broad strands:

- support for the pupil
- support for the teacher
- support for the curriculum
- support for the school.

Although an assistant may be given specific responsibility to support an individual pupil, it is important to remember that assistants will also come into close contact with many other children and it will be important to support and work with the individual pupil alongside or within a group of pupils during lesson times, so that the support given will in practice extend to other pupils in the class.

Assistants will regularly be working alongside a teacher and, depending on the school setting, this may be principally one class teacher or at secondary level a number of different teachers.

Assistants now regularly deliver 'catch up' programmes, e.g. Early Literacy Support or Springboard, from the literacy and numeracy strategy to groups of pupils. They also support the teacher by contributing to the planning for pupils with special educational needs and in helping to assess and monitor pupils' progress on learning and behavioural targets. Assistants routinely support pupils with special educational needs in a range of curriculum subjects, including literacy, mathematics, PE, science and ICT.

In many schools and pre-school settings assistants make a major contribution to the school or setting as members of a team. They participate in extra-curricular activities, helping to enrich the quality of school life. Assistants are also essential to the successful implementation and maintenance of school policies and practices. Because of the wide contributions assistants can make, it is particularly important to be clear about roles and responsibilities.

Every teaching assistant should have a written job description. It should describe the range of duties that will be required. The job description should indicate if the job is to support an individual pupil and if so what proportion of the assistant's time will be in supporting that pupil and what proportion will be either supporting other pupils or performing other duties.

Job descriptions will often be generic rather than detailed and specific because of the nature of the work. Flexibility is essential both in the nature of the tasks and in attitude to the supporting role. It is very hard to predict and be specific about every aspect of support a pupil may need, so assistants need to have a flexible and practical approach in trying to ensure that the needs of pupils are met in a wide range of situations.

Working with the SENCO

In many school and pre-school settings it will be the SENCO who line-manages the assistants. This may not always be the case; in some schools it may be the head teacher or a member of the senior management team. It is the SENCO who is responsible for the day-to-day management of SEN provision in a school. He or she will usually be responsible for ensuring that individuals and groups of pupils with special educational needs receive the support that they need. The SENCO must ensure that statemented pupils receive the appropriate level of support together with the additional and different provision that is specified on the pupil's statement of special educational needs. The SENCO is also responsible for monitoring that the SEN provision is effective and that pupils with SEN are making adequate progress.

The SENCO will also be responsible for ensuring that both teaching staff and assistants receive the training that they need to ensure that the pupils' needs are met. As an assistant it is important for you to ask for training if you do not feel confident to meet the needs of individuals or groups of pupils that you work with. It is also very helpful to let the SENCO know of any special skills or experience that you may have. The SENCO will plan and organise training in different aspects of special educational needs and this will include training specifically for teaching assistants. If you have a particular interest or wish to extend your own professional development, the SENCO is likely to be able to help you.

The SENCO may ask you to contribute to the Annual Review of any statemented pupils whom you support. You may be asked to comment on a pupil's progress and in some cases on their motivation and self-esteem.

Assistants are also frequently asked to contribute to the reviews of IEPs for pupils at School Action or School Action Plus.

The SENCO should ensure that you know the policies and procedures that are operated in the school. These will include general school policies, fire drills and how pupils are expected to behave. Understanding the procedures concerning confidentiality will be particularly important. Assistants will also need training on aspects of the national literacy and numeracy frameworks, the structure of the literacy hour and the daily mathematics lesson. Assistants will also need to be informed of school procedures for registration times, playtimes and lunchtimes, etc.

The SENCO or the head teacher is responsible for ensuring that there are clear guidelines for both assistants and teachers on how they should be used in the classrooms. This means that there will be a variety of roles and duties which assistants can undertake and the planning with the SENCO and/or the class teacher will indicate the most appropriate role for the assistant in different lessons depending on the needs of the pupils being supported.

Working with the class teacher

Most assistants working in early years settings, primary or special schools will be classroom based, working with one or two teachers. Assistants in secondary schools may work alongside a number of different subject teachers or will be attached to a curriculum department, supporting a number of different students in a particular subject.

A new or inexperienced assistant may feel apprehensive about working with an experienced teacher who may not be used to having an assistant in the classroom. In the same way young and/or inexperienced teachers can feel intimidated by a more mature and/or experienced assistant in the classroom. Mutual trust and respect needs to be developed and this can be promoted by discussion between the assistant, the class teacher and sometimes the SENCO to establish the roles and responsibilities of each, and by agreement to discuss any issues as they arise. The teacher will be responsible for planning and directing the assistant to support a pupil or small group in each lesson. The amount and type of support needed may vary from lesson to lesson. The teacher will need to explain the expectations for each lesson and should ensure that the assistant is familiar with the teaching methods and any resources that will be used in the lesson.

In practice teachers and assistants usually develop extremely positive working relationships, but there needs to be sufficient time allocated for the class teacher and the assistant to meet together to plan lessons and to discuss and evaluate the outcomes. Assistants have an invaluable role in ensuring that the teacher is informed about pupils' progress and responses to lessons or intervention programmes. If there is a good dialogue between the class or subject teacher and the assistant, it is much easier to achieve appropriate differentiation and support and this will enable the pupils to make more progress. For example, if a pupil has found a particular reading book too challenging or too easy, the teacher needs to know so that a more appropriate text is used the next time.

Planning and liaison between teachers and assistants is essential. Assistants should be familiar with the pupils' IEPs and the individual learning targets and the resources and strategies that will be used to support the progress towards the targets. Planning will be more effective if the assistant is familiar with the progression of the curriculum targets; for example, if a TA is familiar with the progression of the word level targets in the literacy strategy, it is easier to check and make sure that pupils with special educational needs are secure and have opportunities to revisit and practise earlier targets to ensure they do not lose or forget them.

It is important that both the SENCO and the teachers working most closely with the assistants help them to develop a clear understanding of the learning progression in various curriculum subjects. Planning sessions between teachers and assistants need to include not only what has to be taught and learned but also how the learning will be achieved. Sometimes teachers may assume that assistants will automatically know what strategies to use and will have a range of them at their fingertips. Assistants should be clear and confident about how to support a pupil most effectively and should seek help and advice when necessary. It is equally important that where an agreed approach is working well, or appears not to be working, the information is fed back to the teacher. In reality, the time constraints on teachers and assistants often severely limit quality planning and liaison time, so it is important to agree the best way to ensure good communication. Some schools will have a whole-school policy in which assistants will feed back to teachers through a specific record-keeping procedure. In other schools it may be up to individual teachers and assistants to agree the best way to liaise about pupil progress and lesson planning.

Working with other professionals from the local education authority

All LEAs will have a range of support services that work with schools and parents to ensure that the special educational needs of pupils with more severe and/or complex difficulties are met and that the achievements of pupils with SEN are raised.

Educational psychologists

All local authorities have an educational psychology service. Services in different authorities may work in slightly different ways. In most services, an educational psychologist (EP) will visit schools routinely to discuss and advise on SEN provision and learning support in schools. They may discuss and be involved in individual cases where pupils' needs are more severe or complex or when an individual detailed assessment is necessary. EPs also have a legal (statutory) duty to assess the needs of pupils as part of a multi-disciplinary assessment which may lead to the issuing of a statement of special educational needs. Educational psychologists, when visiting a school, will usually work with the SENCO, the head teacher, the class teacher and the parents. In order to make the EP visit as effective as possible, schools are often asked to provide information about an individual pupil. In many cases, it is class teachers and assistants who are the most appropriate people to be able to give detailed information about a pupil's learning progress or behaviour in school. As an assistant you may be asked to give the EP information or to discuss a pupil's needs.

As an outcome of the EP's visit you may be asked to keep a particular type of record of the pupil's behaviour or learning. The EP may also advise on the use of a particular teaching or support strategy to help a pupil make progress. In many cases it will be an assistant who will actually put the strategy into practice or carry out the recommended intervention programme with the pupil. As an assistant you may be the person who has the most direct contact with an individual pupil. You may be the best person to feed back to the EP on the progress a pupil has made on the intervention programme. In order to feed back accurately and objectively, you will need to keep records of the interventions and the pupil response or progress. So it is important that you agree with the EP and your SENCO the format of the records and exactly what information needs to be recorded.

Specialist support services

Most LEAs have a range of specialist support services to help schools to meet the needs of the pupils who are at School Action Plus or have a statement of special educational needs. The services usually include teachers with specialist training and knowledge in teaching pupils with hearing impairment, visual impairment, behavioural, emotional and social difficulties, autistic spectrum disorders and language impairment. Some authorities may also have services for pupils with general learning or specific learning difficulties.

Many special schools now provide an outreach service for mainstream schools where teaching staff from special schools will visit mainstream schools to give advice on meeting the needs of individual pupils.

Most SEN support services will provide a range of services to support schools in meeting the needs of these pupils. This may involve a specialist teacher observing a pupil working alongside a teacher in the classroom, modelling the teaching of a lesson, or using a particular teaching strategy or resource. In some cases specialist teachers may carry out an individual assessment which involves observing the pupil in the classroom and working with him/her in the classroom or individually. Assistants can often provide invaluable information about the pupil's needs, his/her learning preferences, skills and areas of difficulty.

Specialist advisory teachers will not only give advice, they will often demonstrate particular strategies or will model how to use a specific resource. It is important that the assistants working most closely with individual pupils know what the pupils' learning targets are and are confident in using the strategies and resources that will be most effective. Advisory teachers will also need records of the pupil's progress in order to assess the effectiveness of the strategies and interventions being used. They will often advise on how to record the intervention and the outcomes or provide a proforma record sheet to help with the recording.

Working with professionals from the health service

For some of our pupils with the most complex needs, it is essential that their medical and health needs are met alongside their educational needs. For many pupils there will be a combination of health and education professionals working collaboratively within a school setting. There are a number of professionals from the health service who will visit schools to advise or work directly with individual pupils.

Speech and language therapists

Speech and language therapists are sometimes employed directly by special schools where they work with the school staff on programmes for pupils with severe or profound difficulties to overcome feeding and swallowing problems as well as on developing both speech and language skills.

Increasingly speech and language therapists are working within schools, particularly in schools where there is a high incidence of delayed or impaired language development. Many assistants are now receiving training from speech and language therapists in order to become confident in delivering language development programmes on a regular basis for individual pupils. The therapist will also advise on how to keep the relevant records to monitor the pupils' progress.

Physiotherapists

Paediatric physiotherapists work with children with some of the most complex needs, those who have general developmental delay, disability or illness. Physiotherapy may need to be delivered at home or at school. Physiotherapists often work within special schools and mainstream schools to support pupils with physical and/or medical needs. They will assess pupils' needs and may carry out regular therapy for those pupils who need to develop their gross-motor skills. For some pupils this may be developing the ability to sit, stand or walk. They will also advise and train school-based staff and parents to carry out the daily therapy that individual pupils may need in order to maintain and develop gross-motor skills.

Physiotherapists will also advise and train school-based staff to carry out the daily therapy needed by some pupils, such as children with cystic fibrosis who need daily physiotherapy to prevent the build-up of mucus in the respiratory tract. They help with planning appropriate differentiation of the curriculum and differentiation in lessons such as PE to enable pupils to participate as fully as possible in all aspects of school life.

Occupational therapists

Occupational therapists focus on developing the skills needed to become independent in daily living. These include self-help skills such as dressing and eating and also educational skills such as handwriting. They may work directly with children in pre-school or school settings, or they may advise school-based staff on implementing individual programmes, or on the use of suitable resources that will support the pupils' progress.

Assistants are often the persons most frequently involved in the daily implementation of a programme or in the use of specific resources.

Nurses

Pupils with the most severe and complex needs may also need nursing care within a school setting. This is usually provided by children's community nurses or school nurses.

School nurses provide advice and training to school staff on the care and support of pupils with medical needs (which are discussed in Chapter 12) to ensure that their day-to-day needs are met and staff are trained in any emergency procedures. Nursing advice and support is also given to pupils who need interventions, such as feeding through naso-gastric tubes, catheterisation or care for comfort. For many children with multiple and profound difficulties, a nursing care programme will be planned and monitored by the community or school nurse, but the intervention may be delivered by an assistant who has been trained by nursing staff. The school-based staff will keep in close communication with the nursing services in monitoring and evaluating the pupils' needs.

Connexions

Connexions is a multi-agency service which offers support and guidance to pupils aged 13–19 years, including those with special educational needs. The Connexions service provides personal advisers who give advice on training and work opportunities which will meet the individual needs of young people as they progress from the education system into the wider world.

Pupils with a statement of special educational needs will have a Transitional Review of their statement when they are 14+ years old (Year 9). The Transitional Review must be attended by someone from the Connexions service, usually the personal adviser. The outcome of the Transitional Review meeting is a Transition Plan for the individual. This will set targets for the pupil to enable him or her to plan for the future, when they will no longer be of statutory school age. Assistants will contribute to the meetings by providing records of the pupils' progress, their strengths and weaknesses. Where appropriate, assistants may be asked to attend the meeting to contribute to the planning for the young person.

5 Supporting pupils with general learning needs

Everyone has learning needs. We all have differences in how we like to learn and how we learn best. We all have strengths and weaknesses, things we find easy and are good at and things we find more difficult. Within any class there will be pupils who have a range of learning needs. Individuals will also have differences in how they learn best and the rate at which they learn. It has been estimated that up to 20 per cent of all children will have some kind of mild learning difficulty at some time during their school career. The needs of most pupils with mild learning difficulties will be met by teachers through careful lesson planning and adapting their teaching styles to suit the pupils' needs.

As an assistant you will be asked to help either individuals or groups of pupils who need additional support to access the curriculum, or to help deliver a specific intervention programme designed to enable them to make progress.

What are general learning difficulties?

Moderate learning difficulties

Pupils described as having moderate learning difficulties (MLD) often have general learning needs that affect a wide range of skills. They will learn at a slower pace than other pupils of the same age and may be generally immature for their age. In recent years pupils with moderate learning difficulties have been successfully included in mainstream schools. Previously they often attended special schools but they can benefit from mixing socially and learning alongside their peers at their local schools. Assistants play an essential role in supporting pupils with moderate learning difficulties in both special schools and mainstream schools.

Pupils with moderate learning difficulties often need support across a range of skills which may include

- memory and reasoning skills
- using expressive language and understanding language
- problem solving and understanding new concepts or abstract ideas
- literacy and numeracy skills
- applying what is learned in a range of different situations.

How can I support pupils with moderate learning difficulties?

As already mentioned, children with moderate learning difficulties may be generally immature in their behaviour, social skills and learning. The teacher when planning for individual pupils may have to track back to the learning targets for younger pupils, possibly to targets below Level 1 (Level 2 is the level of attainment generally expected of most seven-year-old pupils). You may hear teachers refer to 'P scales' or 'P targets'. These are the curriculum guidelines for pupils working below Level 1 in the National Curriculum (DfES 2001c, 2002). The targets break down the learning objectives into the pre-skills that are essential to the development of a range of more complex learning skills.

As an assistant you may be asked to support those pupils with learning difficulties who are working on targets that most other pupils have achieved at a younger age. Not only will pupils with learning difficulties make slower progress, but also the stages of developing their learning will be in very small increments. They will learn best by doing things and will need many opportunities to practise and develop new skills, to develop accuracy in what they do and also fluency; that is, being able to do something with minimal hesitation and as automatically as possible.

Pupils with general learning difficulties often have to spend a lot of thinking effort to do things that we as adults take for granted. Writing tasks involve the coordination of fine-motor movements, expressive language skills (being able to speak or think what you want to say), memory skills (holding a sentence in your head), handwriting skills (holding the pen and moving it correctly) and being able to spell the words. It is easy to understand that things can go wrong at any stage in this complex sequence and prevent the pupil being able to write what he/she wants to say. A particular difficulty in any one of the skills in the sequence will affect the outcome.

Pupils will need encouragement to think about what they need to do and support at various stages to achieve it. Small improvements should be encouraged and praised. It is important to praise pupils and in doing so indicate to them the elements that went well.

Severe learning difficulties

Children described as having severe learning difficulties (SLD) usually have very limited general ability and will learn at a much slower pace than other pupils of the same age. They may also have associated health or medical needs which will affect the rate at which they are able to make progress. They generally require a higher level of support and may need teaching and support to develop social and self-help skills such as dressing, toileting and feeding. These are areas where the younger children in particular are likely to need your help to develop independence.

For many of the younger pupils with severe learning difficulties the teaching focus will be on developing skills which are essential for living and learning and making sure that pupils can access the curriculum.

Generally pupils with severe learning difficulties will have similar needs to those with moderate learning difficulties so that many of the same strategies will be appropriate. Pupils with severe learning difficulties can make considerable progress during their school careers in all areas of self-help, social, and literacy and numeracy skills but are likely to need support as adults and some may find it difficult to live independently.

When you are working with pupils with severe learning needs it is important to remember that although progress may be slow the children *can* learn. The skills that they develop in school and at home will often be essential to enhancing the quality of their lives. Children with severe learning difficulties find it difficult to transfer what they learn in one situation to another situation, so much of their learning needs to take place in a variety of real-life situations. They will need to focus on practising and developing social skills and self-help skills that they will need in their everyday lives. They will need many different experiences in order to slowly develop the confidence and appropriate skills for a wide range of situations. Developing language skills and the use of signs (where it is appropriate) will also be a major focus. You may need to work with pupils following the advice of the teacher or speech therapist on language development programmes to develop individual language skills. The use of signing helps to promote communication and understanding. You may be asked to undertake training to learn signing or symbols systems such as British Sign Language or Makaton.

Children with severe learning difficulties will need multi-sensory methods to help them retain what they learn, but for some pupils language development is particularly delayed and they may learn better using visual methods. This is particularly true for pupils with Down's Syndrome.

Profound and multiple learning difficulties

The needs of pupils described as having profound and multiple learning difficulties (PMLD) are severe and complex. The children may also have high levels of medical needs and sensory impairments that limit their hearing and/or vision and ability to respond to the environment. Children with PMLD are usually dependent on high levels of care and support both at home and in school. The nature of their difficulties means that a range of professionals will be working alongside teachers and assistants in schools. They will usually need help with their physical needs, toileting, feeding, dressing and developing gross-motor skills.

Much of the support for pupils with profound and multiple learning difficulties is very multi-sensory to enable the children to become aware of the environment surrounding them and to respond and begin to communicate with other people. Learning often takes place best through the use of all the senses: visual stimulation, hearing sounds, touch, taste and smell. PMLD pupils may also have sensory difficulties so that teaching will need to focus on the use of a specific sensory input.

Strategies to support pupils with general learning difficulties

Strategies to support pupils with poor short-term memory

Pupils with learning difficulties often have very weak short-term memory. Pupils with poor short-term auditory memory (difficulty remembering what they hear) will find it difficult to retain spoken instructions or information. It is important to remember that for many pupils their short-term memory is so short that within seconds there will be no trace of what they have just heard. Just think what happens when you are trying to remember a telephone number and someone speaks to you before you can write it down. If you cannot keep rehearsing the number by saying it to yourself you lose it and however hard you try you cannot remember the number. In the same way children with poor short-term auditory memory will not be able to recall what they have been told despite encouragement with phrases such as 'try hard to remember'. They just will have no memory trace. So they need strategies to help them retain the information for as long as possible to enable them to respond appropriately.

As an assistant you can help by using some of these strategies:

- Give short concise instructions one at a time
- Ask the pupil to repeat the instruction
- Allow time for the child to process the information and to respond
- Repeat instructions given to the group or class to individual pupils
- Use visual prompts such as pictures or symbols that can support oral instructions given by the teacher and act as a reminder
- Repeat instructions or prompt individual pupils at stages throughout a task.

Strategies to support pupils with a short concentration span

- Plan with the class teacher how tasks can be broken down or differentiated so that they can be attempted in short stages
- Discuss with the teacher how a task can be achieved in ways that match the way the pupil learns best
- Ensure that you are well positioned to be able to prompt a pupil to stay on task but not necessarily sitting next to him or her all the time
- Encourage a pupil to sit still by having a special mat or chair to sit on during whole-class sessions in the literacy hour and/or the daily mathematics lesson
- Sit pupils near other pupils who will be good role models for behaviour and learning
- Use visual prompt cards (a card with a picture of an ear or a pair of eyes) to remind the pupil to look and listen during whole-class sessions
- Use a timer to time set targets for maintaining concentration and keeping the pupil focused on the task.

When setting time targets remember to set realistic targets that the pupil can achieve. If he/she can only sit still for one minute at the present time, setting a target of sitting still for ten minutes would not be realistic, but he/she may be able to achieve sitting still for two or three minutes. In this way the length of time can be gradually increased until the pupil can sit still along with the rest of the class for the whole-class teaching session.

Supporting thinking and reasoning skills

Children with learning difficulties often have difficulties with planning and organising themselves. They may need prompting or reminding of what they will need to do next or what they did in the previous lesson. Visual or pictorial timetables can help pupils plan and be prepared for activities or lessons. What a pupil can retain may fluctuate on a day-to-day basis. They will learn more slowly than their peers and will need frequent opportunities to practise or repeat activities until they have mastered a new skill sufficiently to an independent level or are able to consistently remember new information. Children learn in stages, so they often can master a piece of learning but then need many opportunities to practise before they are able to do it accurately and fluently, or they need many opportunities to put what they have learned into practice in a variety of situations. They may need help to recognise the different situations in which they can use what they have learned.

Using a multi-sensory approach

We know that all pupils have different learning styles. This means that some pupils learn better through listening, some are more visual learners and remember better the things that they see. Many children learn more effectively by doing things which combines the use of all the senses. We know that many pupils with learning needs have visual or hearing impairments which will affect the way they learn best. It is always helpful to check that pupils do not have any visual or hearing difficulties and to try to adapt the teaching strategies used to match the strengths or preference of the pupil.

A multi-sensory approach means using auditory, visual and tactile ways of presenting the targets that we want the child to achieve. For example, when learning the meaning of a new word, the pupil needs to hear and say the word, see and read the word, see and handle the real object or, if it is a verb, carry out the action or observe a demonstration of the action. Wherever possible concrete objects and practical materials should be used and pupils should also have as many opportunities as possible of 'doing' or carrying out an action or activity in a range of situations.

Talking a child through a sequence of movements or a process and encouraging them to verbalise what he/she is doing and what he/she will do next helps sequential memory and learning. It also often helps maintain control of fine-motor movements.

At the end of an activity or piece of work it is important to give praise for the effort that has been put into the activity as well as the success of the outcome. You may need to feed back to the teacher if any aspect of a task seemed particularly difficult for the pupil to achieve.

All pupils, not just those with learning difficulties, need to become aware of the strategies that they use in attempting a task and to judge how well the strategies work. It helps to reflect on what went wrong and what needs to be changed next time, e.g. 'The sentence you wrote had some words missing so you need to remember to read the sentence and check that it makes sense and that you have not left any words out.'

Strategies to support the retention and generalisation of what is learned

Children with general learning difficulties, particularly those with more severe learning difficulties, often find it difficult to generalise what they learn. That is, they can do a task within a particular lesson but find it difficult to recognise when to use appropriate strategies in different situations; for example, they may find it difficult to use measuring skills learned in a maths lesson in a science or technology lesson.

As an assistant it is important to help pupils to recognise similarities and differences and to talk to a pupil about applying the same strategy in a different situation. For children with learning difficulties it is essential to point out to a pupil or remind them what the specific targets are on their IEP and to help them to recognise the targets in a variety of situations.

This is particularly common in learning new reading or spelling vocabulary when the words occur not just in the pupil's reading or spelling book but also in text outside literacy lessons. Because pupils with learning difficulties often have poor short-term memory it is helpful to remind them what was taught or practised earlier in the day or in the previous lesson. Again this helps the pupil to focus on the learning targets for each lesson or teaching session.

When supporting pupils in a lesson you may need to prepare them and to focus their thinking at the start of a lesson by reminding them what was covered in the previous lesson. You can use questions to prompt the pupils' recollection of the previous lesson rather than just telling them. Where pupils have individual learning targets it is helpful to remind them of their targets and to point out the different situations in which their targets may occur. Where targets involve learning or memorising information, e.g. reading or spelling vocabulary, pupils will need to over-learn; that is, to practise the targets for short periods. It is more effective to practise very frequently, e.g. at least three or four times each day for five to ten minutes rather than for thirty minutes two or three times a week. It is beneficial to encourage the pupil not only to verbalise what he/she is doing but also to talk about why he/she is learning to do it and how the activity can help them to achieve longer-term goals.

6 Supporting pupils with specific learning difficulties

What are specific learning difficulties?

Not all children with learning difficulties show the delay in all areas of development and the slower rates of progress in all areas of learning that are typical of pupils with general learning difficulties. Some pupils only have difficulties in quite specific areas of development or in particular areas of the curriculum. There are pupils with specific learning difficulties relating particularly to the development of literacy and fine-motor coordination. These difficulties can range from mild to severe. In the more severe cases the development of certain skill areas is slow and requires a lot of effort from the pupil and much support.

When we refer to pupils with specific learning difficulties we are often referring to pupils who may also be described as dyslexic or dyspraxic.

What is dyslexia?

The term dyslexia is used in referring to pupils who have persistent difficulty in developing literacy and/or numeracy skills, in particular fluent, accurate reading and/or spelling, despite receiving appropriate teaching and learning opportunities. Some pupils have specific difficulty in learning some aspects of mathematics.

Pupils described as dyslexic do not all have exactly the same difficulties and the extent of the difficulties varies from mild to severe in different people. Individuals may need different levels of support in different curriculum subjects.

In younger children the indicators that they may have dyslexia include

- difficulty in developing expressive language skills
- difficulty in remembering nursery rhymes or songs
- difficulty in following a sequence of instructions
- difficulty in linking speech sounds (phonemes) with the letter symbols (graphemes)
- weak fine-motor skills in writing, using scissors, etc.
- not knowing the difference between left and right.

Many dyslexic pupils have particular difficulty with what is described as 'phonological processing'. This means that they find it difficult to identify the individual sounds (phonemes) that make up words and cannot easily make the links between the sounds we say and the letters (graphemes) that we write to represent those sounds. English has an alphabetic system of writing and the ability to link sounds in words to letter symbols is crucial to the development of literacy skills. We need to represent the 44 phonemes we use in our spoken language but there are only 26 letters in our written alphabet. This is one of the reasons why we have so many variations and apparent inconsistencies in the English spelling system, e.g. the sound *f* can be written

f as in fish
ph as in graph
gh as in cough
ff as in stiff.

Many dyslexic pupils also have problems with short-term memory. This can be auditory memory, which is the ability to store and retain information that is heard, or visual memory, which is the retention of information that we see. The short-term memory is a temporary store for information from where we can access information and then use it to perform a task or action straightaway or the information is transferred into long-term memory and can then be accessed at a later time. So pupils with short-term memory difficulties often forget instructions they have just been given or may not remember what work was done in the last session. This is not because they are being lazy or not listening; it is because their short-term memory is so limited that they have lost access to the information before they can do anything with it. They often forget the order or sequence of information such as days of the week, months, counting.

Pupils with a poor short-term visual memory will find it hard to retain visually presented information (pictures, diagrams, writing). In particular they will find it hard to copy writing from the board and will be slow at copying diagrams, maps, etc. Not being able to read what is written makes accurate copying even slower and more difficult.

Older dyslexic pupils may have some of the following difficulties:

- Poor spelling; may show over-reliance on phonics (i.e. spelling a word as it sounds), e.g. 'sed' for 'said', 'woz' for 'was', 'wif' for 'with'
- Writing does not reflect knowledge or ability shown orally
- Reading lacks fluency, pupil may struggle to decode unfamiliar words
- Difficulty in understanding what is read after the first time of reading
- Difficulty in following instructions (may appear not to listen)
- Often disorganised or forgetful
- Difficulty in planning and completing extended pieces of writing
- Specific difficulty in some areas of mathematics, e.g. number bonds to 20; recall of multiplication facts; understanding the differences between addition, subtraction, multiplication and division.

What is dyspraxia?

The term dyspraxia refers to difficulties with coordination and the organisation of movements. Problems with 'getting our bodies to do what we want when we want them to do it' is how dyspraxia has been described (Ripley, Daines and Barrett 1997). Children with dyspraxia are often described as 'clumsy' or 'awkward'. They have particular difficulties with complex tasks that require a high level of coordination, e.g. writing, playing ball games, riding a bicycle.

They may have some of the following difficulties:

- poor posture (appearing to slouch in a chair or when standing)
- awkward, clumsy movements
- poor short-term memory
- poor handwriting
- difficulty writing at speed
- lack of fluency in reading
- difficulty with activities such as running, catching, using a bat and ball
- sensitivity to touch, dislike of certain clothes or foods
- poor organisation, difficulty in planning a complex task
- immature behaviour
- lack of awareness of potential danger
- difficulty with the more complex aspects of dressing and/or eating, e.g. tying laces or ties, cutting up food.

There are some difficulties that are common to both dyslexia and dyspraxia. So in order to support pupils effectively it is more important to know which specific areas of learning present difficulties, rather than whether the child is labelled dyslexic or dyspraxic. Each individual will have a different range of difficulties and different levels of need. The amount and type of support a pupil needs will vary according to the demands of each lesson.

Strategies to support pupils with specific learning difficulties

We have already discussed some strategies to support pupils with more general learning difficulties and these same strategies can be adapted and applied for use with pupils with specific learning difficulties. Pupils with specific learning difficulties will also respond best to multi-sensory teaching approaches, so that they use all the senses – vision, hearing and touch. Pupils with dyslexia and dyspraxia often have short-term memory problems and will need the strategies described in Chapter 6.

Further strategies to support pupils with poor memory skills

You can help pupils to recall sequences of instructions or the next stage in a complex task by these methods:

- Use questions that prompt the pupil to remember the next instruction or the next action that is required rather than just telling him/her what to do, e.g.
  - What equipment will you need?
  - What did you have to do/write first?
  - Are there any words you know you will need to write but cannot spell?
- Encourage the use of a quick plan or list that will act as a reminder of what has to be done and the sequence in which it has to be carried out. This can be in words or pictures or diagrams.
- Ask the pupil to repeat the instruction so that you know he/she has understood the task.
- Before the plenary session of a literacy hour or the daily mathematics lesson
  - remind the pupils of what they have done/found out
  - encourage and help them to make a brief note or prompt card that they can use as a reminder of what they want to say during the plenary.
- Reinforce the teacher's instructions by repeating them at stages during a task.
- Remind pupils of strategies that they may have found helpful in previous lessons.
- Prompt the teacher to ask a specific pupil or group of pupils about their achievements or successes during the lesson.

Strategies to support pupils in the literary hour and the daily mathematics lesson

- Ensure they are well positioned to see and hear the teacher.
- Follow up what pupils have seen and heard by experiences with concrete activities.

- Provide concrete apparatus to support the oral and mental starter, e.g. a personal number line, counters, number square, multiplication square, etc.
- Check that pupils have understood any new or possibly confusing vocabulary that the teacher has used. Remember common words, such as even, mean, odd, order, place, times, root, table, have specific meanings in a mathematics lesson that are quite different from general usage.
- Pupils with specific learning difficulties will often need concrete apparatus to support their learning to build confidence and understanding.
- Pupils with poor memory skills will also take longer to learn new sight words, spellings, number facts, etc. They will need opportunities to over-learn or practise these targets. Over-learning is usually most effective if carried out using multi-sensory methods for short periods, several times a day, e.g. learning how to spell high frequency words by using the Look, Read, Spell, Write, Check strategy.
- Be aware that pupils will each have different learning styles and preferences. Some pupils will be good visualisers and can readily get information from what they see, such as pictures and diagrams, others may be better at remembering from what they hear.
- Support pupils by providing lists of key words or subject specific vocabulary that will be needed in the lesson.
- Make sure that there is easy access to the equipment and the resources a pupil will need for each lesson, e.g. dictionaries, spell-checkers, rulers, word banks.
- Expect to have to support individuals or groups of pupils in activities to develop their phonological skills. This may take the form of delivering a specific programme.
- Use multi-sensory approaches through the use of concrete apparatus, e.g. cards, whiteboards, 3D letters in literacy, and individual counters, number lines, number/multiplication squares in mathematics.
- Encourage pupils to use alternatives to writing where appropriate, e.g. diagrams, mind maps, writing frames.
- Encourage older pupils to make quick notes or write key words on a whiteboard to act as a prompt to answer questions or give feedback in plenary sessions in the literacy hour or daily mathematics lesson.
- Give lots of encouragement to pupils when they are practising or over-learning tasks. Give positive feedback on their progress and encourage the pupil to set him/herself little personal challenges to improve, e.g. to get one more spelling correct next time or to get faster as well as more accurate at doing something.
- Over-learning activities are most effective if they can be done several times a day for a few minutes and in each session you recall what was done/learned in the previous sessions before you start.

Reading

- Make sure the texts you read with pupils are appealing and are of the appropriate reading level.
- Remember that making more than two errors in ten words is frustration level and the text will be too hard for independent reading but could be a shared text or used for a guided reading session or paired reading.
- Some pupils find it more comfortable to read from pastel coloured paper or may benefit from using coloured lenses or filters.

Writing

- Dyspraxic pupils may need to use an angle board (which is made of wood or plastic and raises the writing surface to an angle of 15–25 degrees like an old-fashioned school desk).
- Pupils may need a soft or shaped grip to encourage an appropriate pen/pencil grip with the fingers.
- Foam grips or fatter pens and pencils are helpful for pupils who have a very weak grip.
- Encourage pupils to 'have a go' by using whiteboards to plan or experiment with spellings and letter formation.
- Use different widths of line to help scaffold handwriting.
- Squared paper is often helpful in mathematics as long as the squares are not too small for the pupil to write in.
- Make little books as examples and reminders of word level targets, e.g. 'My book about ai/ay spelling pattern'. On each page write a sentence using a word that contains the pattern.
- Use writing frames with appropriate headings or questions that will help the structure and sequence of the writing.
- Use concept maps and flow charts to help with the planning of longer pieces of writing or revision for tests and examinations.
- Encourage the pupils to think about the things that they find helpful in their learning and to evaluate how well they have done a piece of work.
- Always give plenty of praise and encouragement for the effort that has gone into a task, not just for the success of the outcome.
- Feed back to the teacher the amount of effort that has gone into a piece of work. This is especially important with writing where the output may not appear to reflect the effort involved.

Strategies to develop personal organisation

Many dyslexic and dyspraxic pupils have difficulty organising themselves. At the secondary school the timetable can become a major problem for some pupils. The demands of the school day can be very challenging:

- finding their way around the building to different lessons
- planning and organising the required books and equipment for each lesson
- packing, unpacking and carrying bags of books and equipment which can be extremely demanding for pupils with motor coordination difficulties.

It is helpful to

- make sure sufficient time is given to pupils to write down homework accurately
- set up a 'phone a buddy' system as a back-up method for knowing and understanding homework requirements
- Provide opportunities during school time for pupils to be helped with any problems with homework, timetables, lost property, etc.

More detailed ideas for supporting pupils with specific learning difficulties can be found in *Supporting Literacy and Numeracy: A Guide for Learning Support Assistants* (Fox and Halliwell 2000).

7 Supporting pupils with speech, language and communication needs

What are speech, language and communication needs (SLCN)?

All human beings have a need to communicate and interact with others and with their environment in order to meet their basic needs for food and shelter and their higher order needs for social contact. Communication is a vital part of learning, so children and young people who have difficulties in communication, for whatever reason, tend to have learning difficulties as a result.

Children with speech, language and communication needs have difficulty in understanding or making others understand information conveyed through language. Their acquisition of speech and/or written language skills is noticeably behind that of other children. Their speech may be poor or unintelligible. Children with speech needs have difficulties in producing speech sounds (articulation) or problems with pitch or voice quality. They may stutter or be hesitant in speaking and have trouble in getting others to understand. Children with language disorders find it hard to understand and use words in a meaningful way. They may have a limited vocabulary, use words in the wrong place, or have difficulty finding the right words to use. They may use normal grammatical patterns wrongly or find it hard to express ideas. In addition, they may not understand the meanings of words. This often leads to frustration.

Many of these communication difficulties are very complex and hinder the child's learning firstly in the pre-school setting, then at school. Almost every educational task requires a certain level of understanding and use of language. As Ann Lock (1985), who has done significant work in this field, notes, 'Language is the basic educational skill and children who have difficulty with language are liable to have difficulty with almost everything else. Whatever else they need to learn or be taught, they will need to use language first.' In this chapter we will consider what this means, what the learning implications are, and what you can do to give effective support.

Normal language development

Before we further analyse what is meant by speech and language difficulties, it will be helpful to review how language normally develops in young children. There are two main aspects of language development:

- receptive language (what the child understands)
- expressive language (what the child can say and how they can say it).

In normal children language develops in the following sequence:

Receptive language development	
0–9 months	Child listens and responds to sounds and voices.
9–12 months	Child links speech–sound patterns with a particular object, person, situation, e.g. hearing the word 'ball' the child looks for his own ball.
12 months	Understands labels of familiar objects, e.g. car, teddy.
18–24 months	Generalises labels to similar items and miniature objects, e.g. understands 'ball' whatever colour or size.
2 years	Able to understand two main pieces of information in a phrase, e.g. *mummy's nose.* Understands some verbs, e.g. *brush* her *hair.*
3 years	Able to understand three main pieces of information in a phrase, e.g. *mummy's red shoes*, give *Tom* a *little biscuit.* Understands some concepts, e.g. size (big/little), prepositions (in/on/under), colour.
3.5–4 years	Understands a number of pieces of information in one phrase, e.g. Put the *little ball* in the *red box.*
5–7 years	Can understand sentences of increasing complexity, e.g. The mouse was chased by the cat. Go upstairs and get me your socks, shoes and blue trousers.

Expressive language development	
	Random sounds ↓ Rhythmical babble
5–9 months	First word
10–15 months	Single word stage, e.g. dog, here, car, mummy
15 months–2 years	Two word stage, e.g. that doggy, bye-bye Daddy, more tea, all gone, what's that?
2–3 years	Two to four word stage, e.g. my little teddy, me do it, teddy sit chair, in my shoe, baby is crying, train be going, cars in box, all gone milk
3–4 years	Sentence length and complexity increase, e.g. me go in Daddy's car, Daddy kicked the ball, he's sitting on there, I'm going to Nanny's, Paul is bigger than me, I went to school and I did work, I'm staying inside 'cos it's raining
4 years +	Enlarging vocabulary, perfecting grammar, asking questions, including more abstract words, e.g. promise, borrow

Input and output problems

Some children do not follow this normal pattern of development. They have difficulties in understanding language or in expressing language. It helps to think of this as input problems or output problems. This simple model to explain language difficulties was developed by Elizabeth Sisson, a speech and language therapist (1994a).

 ⟵ Input problems (understanding)

- Attention and listening skills
- Auditory memory
- Information-carrying words
- Vocabulary
- Grammar
- Reasoning
- Sequencing
- Semantics

Output problems (expression)

- Immature vocabulary
- Poorly constructed sentences
- 'Odd' sequencing of ideas
- Poor social use of language
- 'Off at a tangent'

Input problems (understanding)

Attention and listening skills

Some children find it hard to listen (some adults too!) and this is often because they have a limited attention span or they are easily distracted. There could be a number of reasons for this difficulty:

- natural liveliness and activity
- hearing impairment or 'glue-ear'
- emotional difficulties
- Attention Deficit (Hyperactivity) Disorder
- learning difficulties.

Auditory memory

This refers to what children can remember in terms of what they hear – this can be words, music or noises. If children find it hard to remember or retain words and the way they fit together to form phrases or sentences, they are likely to develop language difficulties.

Information-carrying words

These are words in a sentence that the child must understand in order to carry out an instruction, e.g. '<u>wash</u> the <u>cup</u>' has two information-carrying words. If the child can distinguish 'wash the cup' from 'wash the plate' and 'dry the cup', then he or she can be said to understand two information-carrying words (this is at about a two-year level). Some children find it hard to comprehend information-carrying words.

Vocabulary

By the age of five years most children have learned the meanings of many different words and can understand what is said to them. Some children are not able to retain this wide vocabulary and this can be for a range of reasons including under-stimulation.

Grammar

The English language is quite complex in the way it is structured and it can be quite confusing! You may have heard young children applying the normal rules of grammar to irregular verbs; for instance, 'Daddy bringed me my drink.'

Reasoning

Input problems may be related to the child's difficulty in reasoning. They may not understand the function of words or sentences and be unable to distinguish between a joke, a statement, a request or a question. Children with delayed language have very poor skills in verbal reasoning and find it very hard to predict, associate or be generative. As a result they find it hard to respond to more abstract ideas, e.g. 'Why . . . ?' 'What if . . . ?' or 'What would you do . . . ?' questions.

Sequencing

We use many words in our everyday language which relate to sequences; for example, 'yesterday', 'today', 'tomorrow', days of the week and months of the year. These ideas can be too abstract for children with language delay. Even when given a two-part instruction, for instance 'Get your school bag and come and sit on the carpet', they may only remember the second part of the instruction.

Semantics (meaning)

Some children have particular difficulties understanding the meanings of words or phrases. Consider the sentence 'They are eating apples' – which has two meanings! Some children find it difficult to understand complicated language structures or meanings. This is particularly the case for children with Asperger's Syndrome, who have a tendency to take things literally; for example, 'Pull your socks up!' and 'Go to the toilet and wash your hands.' Extra care is needed when speaking to pupils with Asperger's Syndrome.

Output problems (expression)

Limited or immature vocabulary

Children who have had limited exposure to normal language patterns at the pre-school stage come to school at a disadvantage. Bernstein (1961) notes that some children come from homes where the adults use a 'restricted code' of language in speaking to each other. Communication is often through short phrases which are similar in construction. Other children come from homes where adults use an 'elaborated code' of language. Here, longer sentences are used, which are grammatically correct and often have subordinate clauses. Bernstein maintains that the language used by teachers is often the 'elaborated code' and not all pupils are 'tuned-in' to this way of speaking. Obviously these 'codes' are two extremes and these days children have the experience of watching television which may develop their understanding of language to some extent, but early interactive language stimulation has significant benefits for children starting school. That is why sharing books with young children and talking with them as they play is so important. Children who have learning difficulties often have immature vocabulary and require additional support to develop language skills.

Poorly constructed sentences

Some children have limited exposure to properly constructed sentences which provide good 'models' for children to follow. It may be that children learn from poor role models or it may be that despite good role models they have difficulties in putting sentences together correctly; for example, 'No me can do that' instead of 'I can't do that.' Young children frequently have difficulties in using tenses correctly and apply the standard pattern to irregular verbs; for example, 'I goed to the toilet', but the majority grow out of this by the time they start school.

Odd sequencing of ideas

Children with autistic spectrum disorders often have difficulties in sequencing their ideas in a normal way because certain words seem to trigger patterns of verbal expression which seem to the listener to be unrelated but which make sense to the child; for example, 'I've been at the school for one year, up station road and there's a Tesco's and a special offer on Easter eggs.'

Poor social use of language

This is also a particular feature of the language of children with autistic spectrum disorders. These children are not aware of the normal social conventions of language use so do not respond to a 'Hello' or a 'How are you?' in a way which would normally be expected. This is sometimes associated with poor non-verbal social skills such as looking at the person who is talking to you. These children can sometimes be taught these skills which do not come naturally to them.

'Off at a tangent'

Some children, particularly those with Asperger's Syndrome, often find it hard to keep their train of thought focused and so they deviate in their thinking, triggered by words which are associated with other things or events. For example, a child might say, 'I am going on holiday in August on an aeroplane. An aeroplane goes over my school and I go to school on Mondays and I have a cheese sandwich.'

Your role in giving support

The first thing to be aware of is that the child who has language difficulties may have lost confidence in communicating, particularly if they are older and have become aware of their difficulties. Therefore, acceptance and reassurance are the first points to bear in mind. Give praise for any attempts to communicate and accept that it may be genuinely difficult for the child to understand what you are saying or make the response you would want.

Different types of difficulty require different approaches. There are many children in our schools who have delayed language development (i.e. language develops normally but at a slower rate) and who benefit from language enrichment activities. This involves providing new experiences and teaching the words to use alongside these experiences. Other children have problems of disordered language development and these pupils require a more intensive approach using the skills of speech and language therapists and specialised schemes (e.g., Derbyshire Language Scheme, Makaton Sign System, Blissymbols).

Guidelines for working with children with SLCN

- Get the child's attention before interaction. Often listening and watching by the child are required to help understanding.
- Main content words should be stressed and understanding will be helped by exaggerated intonation.
- Gesture or use simple signs to help the child understand your message.
- Use short, clear sentences. Take care not to overload the child's auditory memory capacity, so that they can cope with the number of information-carrying words.
- Talk about objects and activities in which the child shows an interest.
- Talk about actions as they are happening.
- Give the child time to respond. Responding in turn is a valuable skill; try not to dominate the interaction.
- Encourage all spontaneous utterances where appropriate and help the child to feel an equal partner in conversation.
- Do not ask too many questions, because this may discourage communication; balance your talking with comment and description as well.
- Use expansion and extension of the child's utterances:
  expansion – repeat the sentence adding words that were missed out;
  extension – a reply that broadens the focus of attention.
- If sounds or words are said incorrectly by the child, repeat the utterance yourself to show the correct way to say it. This is valuable feedback and should sound natural rather than like a 'correction'.
- Don't try to correct everything at once. Choose a sound, or a concept, to focus on for a week or two.
- No one enjoys being corrected all the time. We all learn best when we feel fairly relaxed, confident and are enjoying the task. Therefore praise the child when his/her speech is clear, or new words are attempted, or longer sentences are tried.
- Make sure the instruction uses vocabulary that the child knows.
- Be aware that things may not be done in the correct sequence – the child may only remember the last word you said!

Terminology

Here are some words you may come across in your support of children with these difficulties, together with explanations of what they mean:

Articulators
Lips, tongue, soft and hard palate, teeth and pharynx.

Auditory discrimination
The ability to listen to a speech sound and recognise it consistently, in isolation and in a sequence of sounds.

Complex sentence
An utterance containing more than one verb.

Delay
Development of speech or language is following normal developmental pattern but there is a time lag.

Disorder/deviancy
Development of speech or language is not following the normal developmental pattern; there is a mis-match of linguistic skills.

Dysarthria
Muscle activity is impaired resulting in a limited and laboured range of imprecise speech sounds.

Dysfluency
A disorder of rhythm of speech, e.g. stammering.

Dyspraxia
The ability to control the muscles for speech is disrupted. The patient aims to say a sequence of sounds and another comes out. Purposeful acts are affected while involuntary acts are not.

Echolalia
Repetition, with minimal change, of what has just been said to the patient, in a context which suggests comprehension is absent.

Expressive language
Language which is spoken as opposed to language that is understood.

Function words
Words whose main function is grammatical, e.g. 'to', 'the', as opposed to content words, e.g. nouns.

Information-carrying words
Words in a sentence that the child <u>must</u> understand in order to carry out an instruction, e.g. '<u>wash</u> the <u>cup</u>' has two information-carrying words.

Language
The result of using or combining meaningful units, i.e. words, signs or other non-verbal systems of communicating.

Language comprehension
The ability to understand what is being 'said' by others or by one's self.

Phonology
Study of the pronunciation system of a language and how the disorganisation of these speech sounds impairs communication.

Pragmatics
The study of language in context, at all levels of language use.

Pre-linguistic stage
A very early stage when the first signs of reciprocal behaviour emerge, on which later conversational development depends.

Semantics
The study of the way meaning is organised in language.

Simple sentence
An utterance containing one verb.

Situational understanding
Where the child uses the context of the situation, or the routine, to aid understanding rather than the accompanying language.

Speech
The result of combining speech sounds into meaningful units.

Syntax
The study of word sequence, or sentence structure.

Voiced sounds
Speech sounds which involve the vibration of the vocal cords.

Voiceless sounds
Speech sounds which do not involve vibration of the vocal cords.

8 Supporting pupils with behavioural, emotional and social needs

What do we mean by emotional and behavioural difficulties?

Emotional and behavioural difficulties (EBD) is a blanket term which includes a very wide range of conditions – perhaps the only characteristic these have in common is that the children experiencing them are both troubled and troubling to those who come into contact with them. The emotional difficulties which lead to interpersonal and social problems range from 'internalising' behaviour, e.g. withdrawal/shyness, depression, extreme anxiety and compulsions, to 'acting out' behaviours (sometimes called conduct disorders), e.g. extreme aggression (to people or property), anti-social behaviour, bullying and defiance. If a child receives inadequate emotional nurturing from the parents or carers, particularly at an early age, then the likelihood of emotional and behavioural difficulties is high. Physical and sexual abuse also increase the likelihood of emotional and behavioural difficulties. Learning difficulties can also cause emotional problems for children. A sensitive educational environment and a curriculum at the right level are necessary.

There are many factors which indicate difficulties of this kind and the vast majority of children, at some point in their school lives, will have some emotional and behavioural problems. Children with special needs of any kind often experience these difficulties as part of their perception of themselves as being 'different'. However, it is when problems persist over a long period of time and become severe and complex that additional support will be necessary.

Pupils experiencing severe emotional and behavioural difficulties may need the support of special schools where small class groups and a high level of adult attention are offered. There are many pupils in mainstream schools who also show these difficulties and schools report increasing numbers of such pupils. Some schools have resourced special provision which usually means a higher level of teacher attention and smaller teaching groups for these pupils, who often find it hard to conform to the demands of a full class. Assistants play a significant part in supporting them and making it possible for them to remain in their local schools. The majority of these children do not achieve what they are capable of in academic subjects at school because no child can learn effectively if he or she is troubled inside and has feelings of worthlessness as a result of their home background. However, that is no reason to give up on them and use the background as an excuse. Several research studies have shown that schools can and do make a positive difference to the life chances of these pupils.

Children are not angels and all experience some disturbance in behaviour patterns as they grow and, indeed, challenge to authority can be seen as healthy and normal – there is a streak of mischievous behaviour in many children which can be interpreted as creative and fun-seeking. Some very successful people (a minority it must be said!) admit to having been really difficult to manage at school, and having found it hard to conform to the demands of authority.

What 'problem' behaviours will I see in the classroom?

In your work as an assistant you will become aware of a range of 'problem' behaviours in the classroom. These will range from mild 'low-level' disruptions to full-blown tantrums or defiance. Assistants who work with children have noted a number of behaviours which cause concern:

- humming
- kicking class furniture
- chair rocking
- pencil tapping
- out of seat a lot (can't sit still)
- poking, pushing, 'interfering' with others
- shouting out
- constant talking, giggling
- taking others' equipment
- lashing out at others
- swearing or shouting
- defiance
- throwing equipment
- damaging equipment or property
- spitting
- bullying
- withdrawn behaviour
- frequent crying
- running away
- hiding
- stealing.

It is important to note that most classrooms are well managed by teachers and most behaviour problems are of a 'low-level' type. It is rare to have major outbursts or fighting in class and if it does happen it is the responsibility of the teacher to react appropriately. If you are working with a particularly difficult child, you need to sit down with the teacher and plan who will do what if a major problem should occur.

What is the child's behaviour trying to communicate?

All behaviour has a reason or a purpose and we behave in certain ways to fulfil certain needs. It is sometimes quite difficult to decide what need the child is trying to express but we have to consider this if we are going to be effective in our work. It is made all the more difficult sometimes because we take the behaviours at face value and do not look behind what we see in front of our eyes.

Perhaps you have had experience of trying to put socks and shoes on a reluctant three-year-old who is shouting, 'I hate you – go away!' Of course, we don't take this at face value but we understand that what the child wants is to carry on playing or sleeping or eating or whatever he or she might have been distracted from.

One of the most basic human needs is the need to communicate. If a child has a learning difficulty which hinders or prevents communication, he or she will use increasingly simple ways of getting their message across (such as that he or she is happy, tired, unhappy or scared). Unfortunately, many of the simplest ways of communicating involve behaviour which the rest of us find unacceptable, such as demanding, swearing or having tantrums. If the child is using these unacceptable behaviours in order to communicate, we can reduce or even eliminate the behaviours by teaching the child a better way to communicate the same message. The trick, of course, is to identify what the message is that they are trying to communicate – this is sometimes obvious, but it can be subtle. If it is not obvious, the best ways of establishing it are through discussion with teachers and trying different ways of working with the child.

Children need to communicate

Self-needs

- Immediate gratification *(I want it now)*
- Task avoidance *(I don't want to)*
- Escape *(I don't want to)*
- Panic *(I'm scared)*

Social needs

- Attention seeking *(Look at me)*
- Power seeking *(I want to be in charge)*
- Escape by avoidance *(Don't expect me to do it . . . I can't)*
- Revenge *(I don't want to be part of this group anyway).*

Here are some behaviours which may need reinterpretation to decide what the child is trying to communicate and what he/she really needs.

The pupil may be described as . . .	but this could be . . .	the need is . . .
Stubborn 'I don't want to'	Low self-esteem and fear of failure	To belong and be seen as successful by the group
Aggressive	Lack of verbal skills – frustration makes him/her lash out 'I want to be in control'	Help with verbal skills Social acceptance
Disruptive	Inability to cope with work Attention seeking	Help with work Positive attention
Unpleasant to others in the class	Feelings of rejection 'I don't feel part of this group'	To belong and be included
Inattentive	Poor concentration skills	Quiet environment and positive attention
Attention seeking 'Look at me'	Attention needing	Positive attention
Stealing (e.g. food)	Hunger Attention seeking	Survival Positive attention

In your work as an assistant you will wear many 'hats'. You will need to put on your 'detective' hat in order to interpret what the child's behaviour means and this will help you to plan your way of working.

'The difficult behaviour is not the problem. It is the solution (for the child). The problem is finding a better solution for the child' (La Vigna 1992). Your role, as an assistant, will be to help the child find the 'better solution'.

Skills to teach children who communicate inappropriately

Functionally equivalent skills

What behaviour could we teach the child in order to communicate their needs more effectively?

Functionally related skills

What else does the child need to be able to do in order to use an alternative, better behaviour to communicate the same message?

Coping or tolerance skills

Life is never perfect – how can we teach the child to cope with frustration, criticism, etc.?

Supporting children with emotional and behavioural difficulties

If 'low-level' behaviour problems escalate and become persistent and cause us concern, we describe children as having emotional and behavioural difficulties. This is when their behaviour is beyond the 'normal' range we would expect to see in children of their age.

In the course of your work as an assistant you will come across a considerable number of children who need support as a result of having social, emotional or behavioural difficulties. The 1981 Education Act recognises that emotional and behavioural needs are special educational needs because no child can learn optimally if they are unsettled or unhappy in school for whatever reason. Sometimes these difficulties are caused by a physical, sensory or learning disability but often they are rooted in difficult home backgrounds. There is usually a combination of factors which come together to cause the child to exhibit signs of emotional or behavioural difficulty. In a recent study of pupils considered to be 'at risk' of exclusion from their secondary schools, all had recent or current traumas in their home life, 75 per cent had poor reading skills and 25 per cent were identified as having quite marked signs of mental health problems (bulimia, fire-setting, etc.).

Establishing a good relationship with the pupil

It is extremely important that you work to develop a good relationship with the pupil or pupils you support, especially if their behaviour is difficult to manage. These children are sometimes disliked by their classmates and excluded from social groups. Every child needs to be valued but exclusion works to make children feel worse about themselves rather than better. If you can build a positive relationship with the pupil and encourage others to do so too, you will be fostering their participation in the social aspects of school life.

You can build this positive relationship by

- showing an interest in the child's interests
- greeting them by name each day
- noticing when they seem upset or worried
- giving encouragement for effort
- finding something positive to say about them each day
- expecting that their behaviour will improve
- trusting them with responsibilities
- using humour to engage their cooperation.

Here are some examples of ways you can work to improve things for the child:

- Settling the child into school by having a quiet chat beforehand
- Sitting close by, so you can spot potential 'banana skins' and prevent difficulties from arising
- Ensuring the child has all the equipment they need so that they can get on without a fuss
- Giving positive attention to keep the child 'on track'
- Reminding the child of a bad behaviour so you can get an idea of what is causing the problem
- Recording good or bad behaviours
- Resolving conflicts between pupils
- Calming situations which are becoming heated
- Monitoring or tracking a child through their day
- Providing a 'listening ear' for pupils who need to talk about their problems
- 'Catching them being good' and providing encouragement for good behaviour.

How can I prevent problems occurring?

In order to prevent problems occurring and to stop escalation of incidents it is important to do some analysis of what causes the difficult behaviour in the first place. Of course, you cannot do anything about the child's home life but you may be able to identify when a 'difficult' day is in prospect by judging the mood of the child first thing in the morning. In this case you will need all your best 'active listening' skills to encourage the child to talk about what might be troubling them. You may be able to provide some quiet time away from the class group for the child or young person to 'settle' before going into lessons. Just noticing that there is a problem sometimes helps: 'James, I can see you are feeling upset about something. Would it help to talk about it?'

You can also prevent difficulties arising in the first place by following some of these suggestions:

- Sit the child next to a well-behaved pupil – sitting him or her next to a 'sworn enemy' is a recipe for disaster.
- Ensure he or she is sitting near the front of the class with few obstacles to pass on the way to his or her seat.
- Ensure the pupil has all the equipment he or she needs.
- Give the pupil tasks and activities which he or she can do – too difficult a task can cause frustration which may lead to disruptive behaviour.
- Give the child 'positive' attention early on in the day. Children who are 'attention-needing' are going to get your attention one way or another – usually this is through the 'negative' attention of being 'told off'. However, if you are proactive in this process and give praise and good messages to the child *before* things start to go wrong, you are more likely to prevent difficulties arising.

Some ideas for supporting children who have emotional or social behavioural difficulties

Take every opportunity to improve the self-esteem of the pupil

Give praise when he or she conforms to normally expected standards of behaviour in school or when he or she achieves something they have never done before. This can be related to schoolwork or to behaviour. Try to 'catch them being good' and let them know why you are pleased: 'Jenny, I like the way you came into the classroom this morning' (behaviour); 'Robert, you've read those words really well today. Well done!' (schoolwork).

All children seek to belong to the group and their self-esteem can be badly damaged if they are excluded by other members of the class. As an assistant you need to encourage other children to accept the child so that he or she is not left out.

Helpful information and workshop activities for improving self-esteem in children can be found in a video workshop pack 'A Bag of Tricks' (Maines and Robinson 1988). There is a useful booklet to accompany the course (Maines and Robinson 1992).

Rewards are very important

Rewards show the child when he or she is succeeding and that it is worthwhile to succeed! Find out what your child values as a reward. Sometimes a word of praise or a pat on the back can be enough, but for many children with emotional and behavioural difficulties you will need to provide more tangible rewards (a wall chart with targets, a favourite game, etc.).

Develop your listening skills

You will be sensitive to the feelings of the pupil if you can listen and observe effectively. If you can encourage the pupil to talk about feelings, it can be helpful. Try to look for solutions to the problems rather than dwelling on the causes. (Ask, 'What needs to happen in order to avoid this situation in the future?) There will be many parts of the pupil's life which you cannot change for the better. Accept this and concentrate on those parts you can change (e.g. self-esteem, patterns of behaviour in school).

Encourage the pupil to take responsibility

Many pupils with emotional and behavioural difficulties find it very hard to take responsibility for their own actions. Enabling them to understand what effects their behaviour has on others is an important step in moving towards changing unhelpful behaviour patterns. Role-play or drama activities can be very helpful in enabling those pupils to do this. If you can give the pupil a position of responsibility in the group this will assist the development of mutual support and social responsibility and it will also foster a sense of trust.

Point out good role models

Do not assume that the child knows how to behave. You may need to teach him or her the behaviour which is needed in school. If you can get the child to copy another child who is behaving well, you will be demonstrating what is wanted. Do not overdo this, however – it can be very bad for self-esteem if it is always being pointed out that others do it right!

Try to anticipate trouble

Learn to recognise those situations in which problems for the pupil commonly arise, e.g. lining up at the door, coming in from break, being late for lessons. Help the pupil to recognise these situations for him/herself and work out strategies for minimising or avoiding trouble. If a pupil can learn to keep out of the way of other pupils who seek confrontation, this can make a tremendous difference to his or her life in school.

Deal with 'bad' behaviour in a positive way

By the very nature of their difficulties, these children will not always behave like the majority of the others and their anxiety or anger will 'spill over' in school. However, when incidents or confrontations do occur, it is important to deal with them in a calm and reasonable way. Remember to label the behaviour and not the child. Calling a child 'stupid', 'naughty', 'bully', 'slow' only serves to reinforce the idea in the child's mind that they are indeed stupid, naughty, bully or slow. The message must be 'I like you but I don't like your behaviour.' It is often helpful to talk about the effects the behaviour has had and the feelings it engenders in others: 'Jane, when you take money from the teacher's drawer it lets her down, and she's sad about that because she wants to trust you.'

Communicating your own feelings about the incident can be helpful: 'John, I feel angry when you mess about because you don't give me your best work and I know you can do better than this.'

Staying calm is very important. If you 'lose your cool' it will only serve to make the pupil feel worse and increase the likelihood of the incident occurring again.

Be realistic

Be realistic in setting goals for the pupil. Don't try to change all 'bad' behaviour at once. Choose one objective to start with (e.g. sitting in seat for five minutes, not shouting out for ten minutes). Be consistent, make it clear to the pupil what you are aiming for and reward the pupil if the target is achieved. Remember that it took a long time for the pupil to learn their patterns of behaviour, and overnight transformations are unlikely.

Planning an individual behavioural programme

You will need to work with the teacher in order to develop an IEP (or IBP – individual behaviour plan) for a child. You may be asked to do an observation of the child in a particular lesson in order to find out exactly where the problems are coming from.

There are a number of points to bear in mind when planning a behavioural programme. It should be:

- **W**orkable – it should make sense to you and the child, with clear targets. It will work best if all adults who work with the pupil (teachers, parents, TAs), are clear about the plan.
- **A**chievable – you should plan it so that the child will be successful.
- **R**ealistic – don't try to change all 'bad' behaviour at once. Start with one thing and work in steps towards success. It should be the right thing for the pupil in the situation, e.g. choosing 'staying in seat' when other children are moving round is not realistic.
- **M**anageable – it should be easy for you to monitor and record results.

The following framework provides a structure for deciding how to support the child. It works best if you can make this plan together with the class teacher and if you both carry it out.

Step 1

Write a short list of those behaviours you want to reduce. Next to these behaviours write the ones you want to see instead, e.g.

Unwanted behaviours	Desired behaviours
Shouting out	Listening / working quietly
Getting out of seat	Staying in seat

Step 2

Do an observation of the child. Become a 'fly on the wall' for half an hour and watch what is going on. Make a chart so that you can record what is happening. This will give you baseline information and provide a starting point. Here is an example of an observation chart:

Observation chart

Name: _____

Lesson: _____   Time of day: _____

time	shouts out	out of seat	'on task'
10.00–10.05	3	2	3 mins
10.05–10.10	2	0	2 mins
10.10–10.15	2	1	1 min
10.15–10.20	0	0	0 mins
10.20–10.25	0	1	4 mins
10.25–10.30	2	2	2 mins
Total	9	6	12/30 mins

From this observation it would make sense to target shouting out as a priority. You may want to share these results with the pupil to agree you are aiming for a zero score but in the first week it might be more realistic to go for, say, six – whatever reduction seems realistic and actionable. You would then explain to the pupil that the behaviour you want is 'keeping quiet in lesson time and raising hand to speak'.

Step 3

Review your list in step 1. You may have noticed other behaviours which become priorities. Decide which particular behaviour you want to encourage, e.g. staying in seat, keeping hands to self, staying quiet and putting hand up to say something.

Step 4 – environment analysis

Now look at what you might do to prevent this behaviour occurring in the

first place. Consider whether you can change the location, peer group, subject or activity, in order to eliminate or reduce the unwanted behaviour. For example:

- If a pupil always gets into trouble when working next to particular child, don't allow them to work together.
- If a pupil starts distracting others shortly after a task has begun, ensure the task is clear and achievable when it is given.
- If a pupil finds it hard to get started on a task, ensure he/she has all equipment necessary before you start.

Make a chart to see what can be changed to prevent the behaviour happening in the first place:

Can these be changed?	No	Yes	How? and By Whom?
Location of pupil: proximity to teacher			
Location of pupil: sitting beside whom?			
Subject lesson			
Task			
TA			
Teacher (e.g. parallel groups)			
Child's physical state			
Child's emotional state			

Step 5 – teach new skills

Children need to be taught how to behave. You may need to demonstrate appropriate behaviour by role-play or by pointing out others modelling the right behaviour. The child may need considerable practice. Role reversal where you play the part of the child, and the child the teacher, can increase perception! For example:

'This is how I want you to come into the classroom' (demonstrate).

'I want you to keep your hands together on the table when I'm speaking' (demonstrate).

'I like the way John has started work straight away. I want you to do that.'

'I want you to keep quiet when I'm talking and put your hand up when you want to say something.'

Step 6

Share the results of your observation with the pupil. Explain that you are going to work together to encourage 'staying in seat', for example, by cutting down the times he or she is out of his or her seat. Ask the pupil what needs to happen in order for them to stay in their seat. Involve the pupil in setting a target for the next similar lesson, e.g. cut down from eight times to four times out of seat. Monitor and check how things are going – 'How's it going?', 'You're doing well', 'You're remembering to sit in your seat. Well done.'

Examples:

Problem behaviour	Target behaviour (positively phrased)
Shouting out	Keep quiet and raise hand to speak
Out of seat	Stay in seat
Distracting others by poking	Keep hands, feet and objects to yourself
Seeking a great deal of adult attention	Work alone for five minutes

Step 7 – positive reinforcement of appropriate behaviour

Negotiate a reward for meeting the target (make the target easy to achieve). Ask the pupil what he or she would like as a reward. Suggest one if he or she doesn't come up with anything realistic. Suggestions for rewards would be:

Infant/Junior

- Bubble blowing
- Decorating plain biscuits with icing and sprinkles
- Extra time on the computer
- A favourite game
- Music while you work
- Certificate to take home to parents
- Special responsibility

Secondary

- Extra computer time
- Pen
- Key ring
- Certificate to take home
- Cooking
- Special responsibility
- Free ticket to school disco.

The lottery principle

It is sometimes even more motivating if several rewards are possible, each written on a card and put in an envelope. One reward should be extra special. The pupil takes a chance on choosing a reward and might get the 'star prize'.

Step 8

If the target is achieved give a reward and praise and record it on a chart for the pupil to see. Set a new target for the next similar lesson, e.g. twice out of seat.

If the target is not achieved, make it easier and say 'We'll try again tomorrow.'

Step 9

Continue for two weeks giving the negotiated reward for targets which are achieved. Review the programme. Continue to make targets clear and to teach any new behavioural skills the child needs and review environmental factors.

Step 10

Do another observation and compare it with the original. Use the same lesson and same time of day. Is there any improvement? If not, why not? Consider appropriateness of task, peer group and environment.

Step 11

Choose another behaviour: 'Now that you're able to stay in your seat most of the time, we're going to choose another target. What do you think we could work on next?'

Remember to keep a written or picture record of what is achieved. The pupils might enjoy doing this themselves, e.g. putting stickers on a chart. Negotiate a 'super reward' for the pupil after two weeks of improvement. Send any good news home to share with parents. Ensure the task the pupil is given is at the right level for his or her ability. Problems often occur when pupils are bored or the task is too hard.

Step 12 – reactive strategy

If you have provided an optimum environment for the pupil, e.g. task at right level, sitting by non-troublemakers, and the pupil deliberately chooses not to follow an instruction, you will need to discuss with the teacher what sanction to apply. The first 'reactive strategy' should be a warning, e.g. 'If you keep on getting up out of your seat, you will be moved away from the group.' Children dislike being moved to sit away from their friends, so this is quite an effective 'mild' sanction. This should only be done for short periods at a time. Evidence suggests that it is not the severity of the sanction but the consistency with which it is applied that makes the difference.

What help is available to the assistant?

The SENCO or head of year may be able to give you help in dealing with more difficult pupils and there are also external specialists, such as educational psychologists and behaviour support teams, who are able to provide guidance and support. You need to know that you are not working on your own but as part of a team and that you do not have the sole responsibility for supporting the pupils. You need to remember that the pupil with behavioural difficulties has taken a long time to learn these inappropriate ways of behaviour and overnight changes are unlikely, but the pupil can learn better ways and you can help them to do this. If you are not clear about what to do and how to do it, a detailed job description is a good starting point. If you don't have one, you need to ask for one. All schools are required to have behaviour (discipline) policies and you will find it helpful to read the one in your school so you know the framework within which the staff operate. It is sometimes the case that assistants are left to manage the difficult behaviour of individual pupils on their own and this can be a problem for assistants. You may need to speak to the teacher or head teacher about any concerns.

Attention deficit (hyperactivity) disorder (AD(H)D)

What is AD(H)D?

AD(H)D is a term used to describe long-term difficulties of inattentiveness, hyperactivity and impulsive behaviour:

- Inattentive means being easily distracted, not being able to settle and being forgetful and disorganised
- Hyperactive means being restless, fidgety and always 'on the go'
- Impulsive means having a tendency to interrupt, talk out of turn or be unable to wait.

AD(H)D is a medical diagnosis. Difficulties should have been obvious for more than six months and before the age of seven years. Some children do not have hyperactive symptoms although they fit the descriptions for being inattentive and impulsive. These children are described as having ADD – attention deficit disorder without hyperactivity. Sometimes doctors prescribe tablets (usually Ritalin) to make children calmer. It seems that some children are born with a genetic make-up which makes them more impulsive than others.

There is some evidence to suggest that other children who develop AD(H)D do so as a result of traumatic, emotional or abusive experiences at an early age. When they have had these extremely difficult times, their awareness of threat or danger in the environment is raised and their physiological arousal levels become higher as a result, making it more difficult for them to settle.

As a result of their difficulties, pupils with AD(H)D find it difficult to plan and control their behaviour. They often seem to be unaware of danger and have a tendency to rush into things. With their seemingly endless talking and activity, adults can find these pupils extremely hard work.

Children with AD(H)D are often of average to high ability, but worry their parents and teachers because their classroom achievement is erratic and frequently below their apparent level of ability. Their classroom behaviour is characterised by some or all of the following:

- Being out of their seat too frequently
- Deviating from what the class is supposed to be doing
- Not following the teacher's instructions or orders
- Talking out of turn or calling out
- Being aggressive towards classmates
- Having a short attention span and being easily distracted
- Bothering classmates by talking to them or intruding on their work efforts
- Being oblivious of what is going on and daydreaming
- Losing and forgetting equipment
- Handing in homework late or not at all
- Handing in incomplete or sloppy work.

These are problems that many children have from time to time. For the child with AD(H)D, however, they are chronic and persistent problems that, while not unsolvable, require more personal effort and resources to address them than are needed by most children. So often, because these problems are considered to be deficiencies in effort and motivation, the constant failures associated with them depress pupils' self-esteem and make them prone to even more failure.

Connection between EBD and AD(H)D

Attention deficit (hyperactivity) disorder is a diagnosis created by the American Psychiatric Association. There are many similarities between AD(H)D and EBD, to the extent that it is sometimes argued that many (possibly 40 per cent) of the children who are categorised as having EBD may well have the AD(H)D condition. Some 3–5 per cent of all children in the USA are estimated to have AD(H)D, and a similar proportion is estimated to exist in the UK. There is currently a large increase in the number of children in the UK being diagnosed as having AD(H)D.

Particular characteristics of AD(H)D that distinguish it from EBD are:

- AD(H)D is considered to be a lifelong condition.
- AD(H)D is believed to have a biological basis, in that it is probably caused by dysfunctions of the neurotransmitters in the frontal lobes of the brain.
- AD(H)D focuses entirely on behaviour.
- An important part of the treatment for AD(H)D is often stimulant medication.

Important similarities between AD(H)D and EBD are:

- Children with AD(H)D or EBD experience difficulty in doing things that other children do relatively easily, especially behaving well. These children do not misbehave from choice.
- Because children with AD(H)D or EBD experience social and educational failure, they often have low self-esteem and do not believe that they are capable of meeting the challenges that they are faced with at school. They therefore become trapped in a repeating cycle of failure.
- There are skills associated with good behaviour, just as there are skills associated with school subjects. Pupils with AD(H)D or EBD need to be taught what good behaviour is and how to conform to it.

Effective practice for children with AD(H)D is often also effective for *all* pupils. Many of the problems experienced by children with AD(H)D are the result of their hypersensitivity to certain undesirable environmental circumstances (especially in schools) that are unhelpful to the vast majority of children.

AD(H)D and medicine

A medical diagnosis of AD(H)D is made by a doctor. It should be stressed, however, that effective assessment and treatment of the condition always involves teachers and parents and, often, assistants in schools. The stimulant medication methylphenidate (brand name: Ritalin) is often prescribed by doctors for this condition. The function of the medication is to help the child to concentrate and thereby take advantage of (for example) learning opportunities in school. If a child's performance is in any way impaired by the medication, it is likely that the dosage is inappropriate and should be reviewed by the doctor.

What are the learning implications?

School is the place where skills in concentration, paying attention and following rules are needed. Pupils with AD(H)D find these skills hard to learn. They find listening to and remembering instructions difficult. They are often out of their seats and distracting to others. Their classmates sometimes find them irritating.

How might the assistant give support?

- Encourage and praise as much as possible
- Make instructions clear and simple
- Use rewards to encourage good behaviour
- Give *immediate* sanctions for poor behaviour
- Be consistent and calm
- Think ahead about possible difficult situations and how they might be managed.

Here are some strategies and ideas to help you in supporting children with AD(H)D as recommended in a book by Paul Cooper and Katherine Ideus (1996). Some of the interventions apply to children with AD(H)D or with EBD, but they seem most effective with children with AD(H)D:

- Children with AD(H)D benefit from concise, clear instructions with as few sub-parts as possible. They should be encouraged to repeat task require-ments back to the teacher, preferably in their own words.
- Avoid repetitive tasks.
- Tasks should be broken down into a small number of short steps.
- Initially, tasks should be relatively short. The length and complexity of tasks should increase only when the pupil has shown success with shorter assignments.
- Academic products and performance, such as work completion, are preferred targets for intervention, rather than specific behaviours, such as remaining in seat. This stresses the need to focus on positive, desirable outcomes rather than the negative, unwanted behaviour.
- Use the 'deadman' test. If a dead person can carry out the behaviour you require it is not behaviour. Behavioural requirements should involve positive behaviours, rather than the absence of behaviour.
- Children with AD(H)D often require more specific and more frequent feedback on their work performance than other pupils.
- Praise and rewards need to be of high frequency. Small and immediate rewards are more effective than long-term or delayed rewards. Remember that children with AD(H)D are easily distracted, so rewards should not be too elaborate or likely to overshadow the task in any way.

- Negative consequences should be clearly focused and highly specific. For example, mild reprimands for being off-task will be most effective when they involve a reminder of the task requirement. Thus it is better to say 'get back to reading page three of your history booklet' than to say 'get on with your work'.
- Preferred activities, such as working on a computer, are more effective rewards than concrete things such as sweets.
- Rewards should be negotiated with the pupil and rotated frequently to avoid loss of interest. Develop a 'rewards menu'.
- Previewing and reviewing of tasks helps pupils to know what is expected of them and to make sense of what they are doing.
- 'Priming' helps motivate pupils with AD(H)D. This involves previewing with the pupil the task and the likely rewards for successful completion.
- Interaction with pupils should be marked by brevity, calmness and quietness. Reprimands, where necessary, should be quiet and accompanied by direct eye contact.
- Children with attention problems are more forgetful than most children. Therefore, it is important to avoid signs of exasperation ('If I've told you once I've told you a thousand times') when repeating task requirements to pupils. Always give task requirements as though you are giving them for the first time, in a calm and measured way. Exasperation will be experienced as unfair by the child with AD(H)D.
- Children with AD(H)D perform better in pairs rather than in groups.
- Difficulties with sequencing and concentration make writing a very difficult task for children with AD(H)D. Alternative means of presenting knowledge, such as through tapes or by writing for them, can help here.

Other sources of information

- The SENCO or LEA educational psychology service
- LADDER (National Learning and Attention Deficit Disorders Association), 142 Mostyn Road, London SW19 3LR
- Parents.

Supporting pupils with autistic spectrum disorders

If you work in a special school, it is very likely that you will come across children with autism or Asperger's Syndrome (AS). More children with these disabilities are now being educated in mainstream schools and it is important that you are aware of the particular needs of this group of children and have some idea of how to manage their special needs.

What is autism?

Autism was first identified in 1943 by Leo Kanner, working in America. He noted particularly that these children seemed to have a real difficulty in relating to other people. The characteristics identified by Kanner have since been modified to provide the key features of autism. These include

An 'autistic' aloofness

This refers to an autistic child's lack of normal interaction with the world around them, and apparent lack of seeking to develop relationships with people, or even to acknowledge other people, other than as objects.

A desire for sameness

An autistic child's behaviour is often primarily aimed at keeping everything the same. They usually respond with extreme distress at even minor changes to their environment or routine. Obsessive behaviours can develop. These are felt to serve a therapeutic purpose for the child, and an increase in frequency or intensity of obsessive behaviours is a sign of increased stress.

A limitation in the variety of spontaneous activity

Linked to the desire for sameness, this exhibits itself in repetitive, monotonous behaviours. A child may seek to impose elaborate routines on their environment, which serve no logical purpose. Children with autism do not explore their world through play, but instead tend to line up or sort toys, imposing order and structure.

Over-sensitivity to stimuli

Many children with autism are unusually sensitive to particular stimuli, including sounds, visual stimuli, smell or taste, as well as touch. A child may be sensitive to a particular pitch or sound, a shape or colour. Sensitivity to smell and taste can affect their eating habits. Over-sensitivity to touch can affect their tolerance of the physical proximity of other people.

Echolalia

Children with autism have significant difficulties in developing language, and some may never develop functional language skills. However, a characteristic of those who do develop speech is to repeat whole sentences or phrases that they have heard, often with the exact intonation and emphasis of the original speaker.

Children with autism are usually educated in schools for children who have severe learning difficulties because they require particular approaches to support learning and to reduce the anxiety which they are prone to. Routine, care and structure are important for this group of pupils. Inability to communicate often leads to frustration and results in behaviour difficulties. If you support a child with autism you will need to work closely with the teacher to implement specific programmes designed to aid communication, e.g. PECS (Picture Exchange Communication System) or the TEACCH approach (The Education of Children with Communication Handicaps).

Asperger's Syndrome

Asperger's Syndrome was first identified by Hans Asperger in 1944 and the term is now used to describe more able children with autistic characteristics. However, there is still some debate about whether Asperger's Syndrome and autism are distinct but similar conditions, or part of the same overall condition. A number of terms are used by various professionals to indicate that a child's difficulties fall into the same general area. The term 'autistic continuum' has been used widely to illustrate that a child's autistic characteristics can range from very severe to relatively mild. More recently, Lorna Wing has introduced the term 'autistic spectrum' to represent the complexities involved in assessing the degree of difficulty in different areas of need. The idea of a spectrum better conveys the fact that each child's needs can differ in severity across a range of skills.

The triad of impairments

Since the original identification of autistic spectrum disorders, there has been much research that has sought a clearer pattern to the difficulties identified by Kanner and Asperger. Lorna Wing recognised that although the difficulties seemed quite diverse, many of the characteristics could be grouped together in broad areas of skill. She categorised the key features of Asperger's Syndrome and autism into three main areas of difficulties, which she called the 'triad of impairments'.

Although children with AS or autism may show additional impairments not covered in the triad, these are not considered essential for diagnosis. What distinguishes autism and AS is the nature and degree of difficulty within the different parts of the triad. For educational purposes, the distinction between the two labels has little impact upon the choice of effective intervention, as what we seek to do in schools is to take into account each child's *individual* difficulties, including the different language needs of each child. An educational approach should also focus on current needs rather than past difficulties.

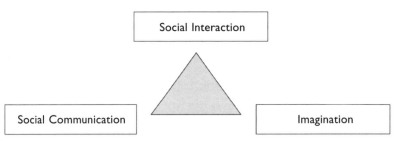

The triad of impairments

Asperger's Syndrome is thought to be a form of autism, and children with AS share many of the characteristics of autism, but in a milder or different form. This does not mean to say that the impact of AS on a child's ability to function is not significant, and it can be particularly hard for the child because much of the time he/she appears to behave normally.

Individual differences in age, general ability, personality, home background and experience will all affect a child's behaviour, and thus the nature of their individual needs. Some children manage to 'hold things together' at school, but the impact of the difficulties they experience may be felt at home, showing itself in extreme anxiety or challenging behaviour. In contrast, some children have more difficulties at school than at home because they are being expected to cope in a more demanding social situation, which provides them with little or no control over what happens to them.

What are the features of Asperger's Syndrome?

Not every child will show all of the difficulties described, or to the degree given in the examples. They may show difficulties in some but not all different situations, or may show more features when under stress.

Social interaction

Impairments in social interaction may include

- Difficulties in interacting with others, especially other children, who can find them odd and awkward in their attempts at making friendships. There is probably less difficulty with adults, because adults are better able to adapt their own behaviour and responses to make the interaction easier and are probably more tolerant of odd behaviour.
- An inability to comply with the unwritten rules of social interaction. They may not be able to adapt their behaviour to a particular context, e.g. knowing that it's all right to talk loudly in the park, but not in the middle of a church service; or that it's acceptable to strip down to their underwear in the garden at home if it's hot, but not in the middle of a supermarket.

- A difficulty in adapting their behaviour towards different people. Some children with AS may be over-affectionate towards everyone they meet, not realising that what is an acceptable response to your mother is not acceptable to your teacher, or a stranger. This is significant in terms of personal safety issues.
- A specific difficulty in recognising emotion in themselves, and in others. Thus they have difficulty in empathising with how others feel, and so cannot provide social support to others in the way that most of us do. They may learn some of the behaviours expected of them in certain situations (e.g. putting their arm around someone who is crying), but do not actually understand the deeper meaning behind the crying or their own learned response.
- Less of an interest than most children in pleasing others and seeking approval. This can cause difficulties in trying to motivate a child, as they may not respond to praise but will require more concrete rewards.
- Because of differences in their understanding of emotion, there may be a difficulty in recognising the importance of facial expression, body language and voice intonation, and the messages that these convey about how another person is feeling.
- A lack of empathy means that individuals with AS do not recognise that what they say and do may upset or embarrass others. They tend to say exactly what they mean without any thought of consequences and do not recognise the need to keep certain thoughts to themselves, or to adapt what they say to avoid hurting someone's feelings. Thus they may quite happily state a point of fact – that someone is fat, or that their singing is out of tune.

Social communication

Although basic language skills appear to be at least average, closer investigation of how the child with AS uses language, and of their actual understanding of what is being said, reveals significant difficulties with the functional use of language. Verbal language itself represents only a small part of what is needed for effective communication, and children with AS can have a range of difficulties in recognising and using the wider methods of communication:

- Literal interpretation of language, so that the child follows what is being said word for word, and no more. This can lead to misunderstanding when instructions or comments can be interpreted in different ways, or when metaphors or colloquial phrases are used, e.g. 'stand on one foot', 'pull your socks up', 'over the moon', 'under the weather', 'take it easy', 'pulling your leg'.

    Some phrases may, understandably, provoke distress, e.g. 'laugh your head off', 'killing time', 'butterflies in your stomach'.

    Further difficulties may be caused in a school setting by instructions which are incomplete, but which assume that the child knows the underlying intention,' e.g.

'Off you go' (meaning 'go back to your tables and start working'),
'It's getting noisy in here' (meaning 'work more quietly').

Certain instructions may elicit a response from the child that makes it seem that they are being deliberately cheeky, e.g.

'Can you turn the page over?' ('Yes'),
'Do you know what this shape is called?' ('Yes').

- When faced with ambiguous or confusing verbal messages, the child with AS does not have the skills to use other cues to interpret the real meaning behind what is being said. Therefore, if they are told 'That's OK' or 'I'm all right', by someone whose body language is actually saying the opposite, they will understand only the words and may, as a result, come across as unfeeling. These difficulties are exacerbated by the fact that we often do not actually say what we mean. For example, when we meet someone we know and greet them with 'How are you?' we don't really want a list of their current woes, but are just being polite.
- Individuals with AS have particular difficulties initiating, sustaining and reporting conversation. They may happily talk for hours about a topic that interests them, but will not take the other person's prior knowledge or interest into account, and may abruptly end the conversation once they have run out of things to say. They find it difficult to apply the subtle rules of listening, reflecting and turn-taking that characterise normal conversation.
- Eye contact is a common problem. In normal communication, we use eye contact to punctuate an interaction, to signify our level of interest, and to confirm joint understanding. Often individuals with AS avoid eye contact altogether, or use it inappropriately, increasing the awkwardness of communication.

Imagination

Difficulties in imagination encompass a range of behaviours that indicate a basic lack of flexibility in the thinking of children with AS, and a tendency to have a limited repertoire of interests and responses. Difficulties in this area may include:

- Symbolic and imaginative play is later to develop, and the extent to which the child engages in imaginative games or activities even at a later age is often limited. There tends to be a preference for factual information over fictional materials. Fictional preferences are for explicit horror stories (which over-emphasise emotions) or science fiction.
- A genuine difficulty in coping with change, sometimes to the extent that they will become extremely distressed when there is an unexpected change in normal routine. This has implications for their reactions when their class is covered by a different teacher, when the times or venues of lessons have to be changed unexpectedly, or when the general school routine is disrupted (e.g. at Christmas time). For some children, even small changes in the layout of a room can cause extreme distress.

- A tendency to become absorbed in particular interests, to the exclusion of other activities. In some cases this can interfere with the child's learning, or with that of others in the class. Interests are often unusual, and commonly involve collecting objects or facts.
- The development of elaborate rituals that do not serve any obvious purpose, other than allowing the child a degree of active control over their surroundings, e.g. having to walk a particular route to school, perhaps touching certain objects on the way; setting out equipment in a specific order before beginning a task.
- A difficulty in generalising skills and adapting what they have learned to different circumstances, e.g. the child who has learned the reception class routine of going to the toilet, washing their hands, and putting their coat on before lining up to go out to play and becomes stuck in that routine – putting their coat on and waiting by the door each time they go to the toilet, regardless of the time of day; the older child who learns a mathematical operation in a maths lesson, but needs to be separately taught the same skill in geography and science in order to apply it in a different context.

How is Asperger's Syndrome diagnosed?

Asperger's Syndrome is normally a medical diagnosis. There is no blood test or brain scan which can do this. It is done by identifying the characteristic behaviours. Some professionals are reluctant to make a diagnosis because of fears about the negative effects of labelling children. However, a diagnosis can confirm in some people's eyes that a child's problems have a genuine root.

It is important for children with Asperger's Syndrome that educational planning takes into account the very specific differences in the way that their skills have developed (or failed to develop). The label of Asperger's Syndrome should be seen as a signpost, or starting point, not a sentence or excuse for inaction.

How can I support a child with Asperger's Syndrome?

Before you start, you need to remember that the responsibility for meeting the needs of a child with Asperger's Syndrome should not rest with one person. As an assistant you will need to work closely with the teacher or SENCO who remains responsible for overall planning and educational development, and any other learning support staff working with the child. It is crucial that all staff working with these pupils have at least a basic level of understanding of the underlying factors that affect the behaviour and learning of a child with Asperger's Syndrome.

So how can you give effective support? As an assistant you will probably need to give support in each of the different areas of need. Here are some practical ideas to help you do this:

Developing social skills

In Asperger's Syndrome, the fundamental difficulty is in coping with the social world, and responding to the behaviour of others. The idea that people with autistic spectrum disorders should be seen as having their own unique *culture* enables us to think carefully about how we target the needs of individuals with Asperger's Syndrome. It is not our job to force normality upon them. To try to do so overlooks the fact that the underlying patterns of thinking are not inferior, but different. What causes difficulty is our expectations. Different cultures have their own unique expectations for behaviour. Within a school situation, many of the situations that we place children in are themselves artificial. Educational intervention needs to focus on teaching those with Asperger's Syndrome new skills in order to help them to cope with our culture and our social world.

Developing play skills

Observation of early play skills in children with Asperger's Syndrome indicates that they differ from those of normally developing children. There is a greater tendency to impose order, sorting and lining up toys, rather than playing with them imaginatively. The development of pretend play occurs later or not at all, and there is often a lack of role-play and social play. It has been suggested that social skills development in children with autistic spectrum difficulties can be improved through direct adult intervention aimed at developing more normal play skills. Intervention could include:

- Playing alongside the child, gently encouraging them to use toys more flexibly and modelling how to use objects in different ways.
- Encouraging dressing up and role-play, through active adult participation.
- Active teaching of play skills following close observation of how the peer group play together, what language they use and which games they prefer. The adult can then act the role of another child in a play situation, teaching the child with AS what to say and what to do. Introduce other children into the games gradually, being careful in your selection of playmates.

Developing emotional understanding

Social skills require empathy, and an understanding of how another person is feeling and what they are thinking. In many cases a child with AS may have learned appropriate responses, e.g. what to do if someone has fallen over, or is angry, but will have no real understanding of the emotions involved. Their actions are mechanical, not empathetic. It can be surprising how poorly some children with AS are able to grasp their own emotions.

Developing the child's understanding of their own emotions

For many children, intervention will need to start at the basics. One way suggested by Tony Attwood (1998) is to help the child to create a collection of things which produce a happy emotion, and link them to outward signs of happiness or pleasure by creating a Happy Book, which is essentially a scrapbook (or even a box) containing

- pictures and photos of things that the child likes
- photos and pictures of smiling faces
- lists or pictures of things that the child likes to do
- favourite colours, animals, music, textures, noises, etc.
- a happy thermometer, or similar scale, that enables the child to indicate degrees of happiness – how happy they are feeling, or how happy something makes them
- pictures of things that make people close to them happy (e.g. mother, father, teacher, friend).

The Happy Book can be used as an ongoing resource to help the child indicate their own level of feeling. It can also be used to help to cheer them up when they are feeling angry or sad. This could be extended to look at other emotions or to contrast feelings, e.g. sad/happy or angry/calm.

Understanding what affects emotions

The book *Teaching Children with Autism to Mind Read* (Howlin *et al.* 1998) is an excellent resource for assessing a child's level of emotional development, and for providing practical activities to develop that understanding. The exercises in the accompanying workbook take the child through the stages of normal development of emotional understanding. This book can be used as a guide for developing emotional understanding for younger children with Asperger's Syndrome. Teaching should be supported by practical activities which draw the child's attention to their own emotions and which focus on the child's own experiences and preferences. Opportunities should then be taken to bring the child's attention to the behaviour of other children that indicates a particular emotion.

Disclosure of emotions

Children and young people with AS, and adults too, find it difficult to identify and share their emotions. This can cause particular difficulties in adolescence when the young person may feel increasingly isolated and not be able to communicate how they are feeling. It is a fact that young people with Asperger's Syndrome are particularly prone to mental health problems and it is not always easy for others to recognise the danger signals.

It is often easier for a child with AS to indicate their emotions through visual means. Regular opportunities should be taken to encourage all children with AS to share their level of emotion, by pointing at happiness thermometers (or similar visual representations). Older children should also be encouraged to express their feelings, and can be given a wider range of faces showing a more complex variety of emotions to select from.

Personal safety

Difficulties in understanding the thoughts and intentions of others can lead to particular problems in understanding the potential danger presented by strangers, or by people not very well known to the child or family. Pupils with AS are particularly vulnerable because their own lack of inhibition often leads to over-familiarity in terms of affection, touch and proximity. It is important that children who are likely to be vulnerable are taught specific rules about what is appropriate language to use, and levels of affection to show to different people. This can be done by getting the child to categorise people into a set of circles of friends, and then setting rules for the child about how to act towards people in the different circles:

Centre Circle	Close family
Second Circle	Special friends
Third Circle	General friends
Fourth Circle	Acquaintances
Fifth Circle	Strangers.

This could also be illustrated to the child through a traffic light system, e.g:

RED	Don't speak to strangers
AMBER	Smiles and chats are OK for friends and acquaintances
GREEN	Hugs and kisses are OK for family.

Teaching social skills

Unlike most of us, people with AS do not acquire an intuitive grasp of social skills as part of their normal development. Instead, specific teaching is needed to explain social situations and to train the child how to interact with others. Many individuals with AS do eventually develop a degree of social skill, but very much at a learned, rather than intuitive, level. Social skills training for pupils with emotional and behavioural difficulties will not always cater for the particular needs of pupils with AS.

Any teaching should focus upon individual needs, and the pattern of difficulties for each child will be different. Careful observation of how the child interacts with others will highlight the particular difficulties that they face, and thus the priority needs for teaching. Often we are simply teaching specific strategies for coping in school situation.

The adult with Asperger's Syndrome at least has some choice about which social situations they put themselves in, and so some of the difficulties that may cause a child or others significant problems at school do not arise in adulthood.

You need to remember these important rules:

- Do not force a child into social situations in the hope that through mixing with others they will pick up social skills.
- Teach specific skills, as far as possible in the context in which they will be used.
- Provide opportunities for the child to practise their skills in safe situations, i.e. with adults and sympathetic children.
- Teach the child specifically about friendships (What makes a good friend? What does a good friend do? etc.).
- Provide positive reinforcements and rewards to encourage the use of appropriate social skills.

Support from other children

Social skills, by their very nature, involve interaction with others. Most children quickly recognise that there is something different about the child with Asperger's Syndrome, and intuitively treat them differently. Many children do their best to help, but can be rebuffed, and this has a negative effect on their own self-esteem. Other children will learn to avoid the child with AS, because they simply do not know how to treat them. Unfortunately, it is also in the nature of some children to exploit an individual with AS because of their very naivety.

There is sometimes a reluctance to involve others in support because of a fear that by doing so we will draw attention to the child with AS as being different, and somehow break a confidence. However, the child's peer group already know that they are different, and will be better able to understand and support them if they are actively involved in thinking of ways to help. As an assistant, your role is really important in encouraging other children to include the child with Asperger's Syndrome and accept their differences as part of the class group.

Supporting positive behaviour

The majority of behaviour problems arise out of anxiety, or not understanding hidden rules of behaviour. Proactive strategies will help to alleviate much of the anxiety and so reduce problem behaviour. These include reducing anxiety and stress by

- Adapting the physical environment
- Providing secure and consistent routines
- Placing appropriate demands upon the child
- Planning ahead for strategies that reduce the likelihood of behaviour problems
- Knowing the child's anxiety triggers
- Knowing the signs of increasing stress
- Anticipating potential areas of difficulty

and responding sensitively to problem behaviour by

- Being aware of the effect of AS on behaviour
- Being consistent
- Staying in control
- Teaching new skills that the behaviour indicates are needed.

Some problem behaviour can arise because specific factors in the environment or situation are causing anxiety and triggering an inappropriate response. It is important to try to identify those triggers so that you can adapt the environment and your own expectations and behaviour. Ask the child, if possible, and consider the following factors:

- The task
- Attention during instruction

- Response to instruction
- Language issues
- Ability to complete the task
- Time spent on the task
- Internal distractions
- The classroom environment
- Potential stress factors
- Potential distractions
- Influence of other members of the class.

Obsessions

- Recognise that obsessions serve a purpose for the child with Asperger's Syndrome
- Provide regular opportunities for engaging in obsessive behaviour, but maintain control for setting aside specific times that reduce the interference with the child's learning or that of others
- Ignore minor obsessive behaviours unless they present a problem
- Don't attempt to eliminate an obsession unless there are significant reasons for doing so. A less controllable obsession may take its place!
- Build academic activities around obsessions
- Use obsessions as a reward
- Monitor the level of obsessive behaviour as an indication of increasing stress.

Maintaining control

Individuals with AS can be very stubborn because of their inflexible view of the world and often egocentric expectations. It will sometimes be necessary to allow the child to apparently get their own way, because confrontation will only escalate a difficult situation. In such instances it is important to follow up incidents with the child as soon as possible, and take action to reduce the risk of similar incidents occurring. This could be achieved through using the Social Stories approach, or Comic Strip Conversations (Carol Gray) to show the child that the behaviour was not appropriate, and to teach new rules or alternative behaviour. These approaches help children to think about particular social situations they find themselves in and to 'learn' the best ways of reacting or speaking to others in these situations.

Where an individual with Asperger's Syndrome attempts to impose their will and refuses to carry out certain tasks, a strict behaviour management system should be introduced to ensure that the adult maintains control. Initially it may be necessary to use a low-demand–high-reward system, so that the child receives a high-value reward for what may seem to be minimal compliance. Gradually, the task expectations should be increased and the reward level reduced. In all cases it is crucial that the reward is truly rewarding for the particular child. Obsessions come in useful here! Sanctions can be applied as for any other child. However, it is important that you first make sure that you have not overlooked an aspect of AS that may be

- preventing the child from achieving their target
- causing anxiety.

Motivation

When working with children with AS it is sometimes hard to find rewards that motivate, as these children are less responsive to praise and attention than most. They are more likely to respond to tangible rewards or tokens, so do bear this in mind when trying to motivate the child you are working with. To provide external motivation, try to ensure that

- the subject interests the child
- the child can see a real purpose to the task
- the purpose of the task is explained clearly in terms of learning gains
- the child has the incentive of a concrete reward for completing the task.

Changing the physical environment

The busy, often cramped environment of the classroom can produce particular behaviour problems for the child with AS. The need for personal space, and particular difficulties with physical proximity, can cause anxiety and lead to aggressive behaviour towards others. Visual distractions can affect the child's attention and concentration. Difficulties can be prevented by

- providing an individual work area to be used for all or part of the time
- placing the child on a group table in a less distracting area of the classroom
- screening off potential distractions
- being aware of potential stress triggers (e.g. noise, glare)
- clear labelling of classroom areas
- allowing the child to leave or enter the room before or after others, to avoid the crush
- allowing the child to use a favourite chair or table.

Providing structure

Much anxiety, which can lead to behaviour difficulties, is caused by the child's inability to cope with waiting, as well as coping with apparently open-ended tasks. The child's concept of time is often not well developed, and this can add to the uncertainty, increasing anxiety levels. You can:

- ensure consistency in your approach
- wherever possible work to a consistent timetable
- provide the child with a visual timetable or work schedule
- give the child as much information as possible about what is going to happen (preferably written)
- give the child warning when an activity is due to change
- prepare the child well in advance for any change in routine.

Some very useful materials to help in understanding and supporting pupils with autistic spectrum disorders have been produced by Lucky Duck Publications www.luckyduck.co.uk

Supporting pupils with sensory impairment

Sensory impairment refers to any impairment of the senses and is mainly of three types:

- Visual impairment (VI)
- Hearing impairment (HI)
- Multi-sensory impairment, e.g. deaf/blindness.

There are now many more pupils with sensory impairment being educated in mainstream classes and many LEAs have special units attached to mainstream nurseries and schools to support these children and young people. However, children with multi-sensory impairments are often those with profound and multiple learning difficulties. Many are very vulnerable and are educated in special schools where specialist care and equipment are available. The incidence of multi-sensory impairment is very low.

Visual impairment (VI)

A survey by the Royal National Institute for the Blind (RNIB) indicates that visual impairment is a relatively low-incidence impairment, affecting approximately two children in every thousand across the UK. Recent research at RNIB indicates that there were some 19,500 visually impaired children in England, Scotland and Wales known to local education authority visual impairment services in 1995. Within this population more than one child in every three was identified as multi-disabled visually impaired, giving a total of approximately 6,700 such children across the UK. Within England, there are approximately 17,000 visually impaired children, at least 6,000 of whom are multi-disabled.

Research shows that five per cent of visually impaired children learn through the medium of Braille. Thus across the UK some 850 children between the ages of 4 and 16 require Braille materials to support their learning and leisure reading. In England alone, there are approximately 700 Braillists of statutory school age. A small but increasing number of children now learn through the medium of Moon, another tactile system, which is simpler than Braille and is more suited to children who have additional learning difficulties. Research during 1997 revealed that in England some 50 children were using Moon. Some visually impaired children with additional disabilities may communicate by other means such as using objects of reference; for example, touching a cup when they want a drink. Data from the RNIB research indicates that around 5,500 visually impaired children of school age require large print, i.e. print of 16 or 18 point size or larger, in order to access curriculum and leisure reading materials.

It is important to note that visual impairment takes many different forms that present in different ways in individual children. A child with one named condition may have different resource needs from those of another child who has the same named condition. Children's needs are individual and may change over time. However, their visual needs will not diminish and indeed may become more severe as the children grow older. Surveys also show the increase over recent years in the proportion of children with VI who go to mainstream schools, with varying levels of support, much of this support coming from teaching assistants together with peripatetic teachers of the visually impaired. About 60 per cent of visually impaired pupils are educated in mainstream schools.

The impairment may be moderate, in which case your work might be mainly concerned with adapting materials and ensuring safety. If the impairment is severe you may need to learn Braille and keyboard skills to produce materials the child can use in order to learn effectively. You may also need to assist the child in learning how to get around the classroom and the school with safety. It is very important to understand the limits of the child's vision.

What is visual impairment?

There are a number of different terms which are used to describe visual impairment:

Blind – this means a person is registered blind under the National Assistance Act 1948.

Educationally blind – means a child/adult has to be educated mainly by non-sighted methods, using touch and hearing only; for example, using Braille.

Functionally blind – describes a person whose main ways of receiving and learning information are by touch and hearing.

Low vision – severely restricted vision, although the limited vision can be used to receive or learn information. Children with low vision may be able to use what sight they have in close-up work with the aid of good lighting, careful positioning and low vision aids (LVAs) such as magnifiers. Braille may also be used.

Partially sighted – describes children who have enough vision for all school tasks but need the help of special teaching methods and materials. Work usually needs to be enlarged so the child can see it clearly.

What are the learning implications?

Sight problems can affect a pupil's ability to do detailed and careful physical movements; often hand and finger muscles are not well developed in pupils with visual difficulties. The usual motivation to explore can be affected by fear, so physical skills and confidence can be slow to develop. The pupil is likely to have less chance to move about and to imitate others and is also likely to have a poor body image. He or she will probably have poor skills involving senses and coordinating movements, e.g. they may find it difficult to pour liquids or to judge distances.

Speech and language should develop normally, but sometimes they are delayed because the pupil has fewer experiences which help develop language. Independent skills are also likely to develop more slowly, because children with poor vision cannot learn by watching. They may not be able to do schoolwork as fast as sighted children and there may also be some difficulties in relating socially to other children. This is because they are not able to learn the meaning of body language or facial expression which other children learn without realising it. Because those around the child may be tempted to over-protect him or her, self-esteem and confidence may be affected and the child may become too dependent on others. A key part of the assistant's role is to encourage the pupil to become as independent as possible.

Opportunities for positive social interaction are important for children with visual impairment. A child whom is worried about whom he or she might play with at playtime may not be able to concentrate on work.

How might the teaching assistant give support?

When working with a visually impaired pupil, your responsibilities are likely to be

- to provide support for the class teacher by adapting teaching materials, e.g. enlarging worksheets so that the pupil can follow the same programmes of work as the other members of the class, or producing materials using Braille
- to supervise the specialist equipment and resources, e.g. magnifying equipment
- to ensure the safety of the pupil and others, e.g. safe use of science equipment
- to support the pupil by helping him or her to learn any special skills, e.g. Braille. You may need training yourself to do this.

You will need to offer support in all areas in which the pupil may be disadvantaged. These areas are:

Orientation and mobility

Clear verbal directions are necessary before any task involving physical movement is attempted. The visually impaired child may not have a visual image of what is required so a visual demonstration is a waste of time; for instance, in PE, if the class teacher is demonstrating, you may need to talk through the steps, e.g. 'Move three steps to the right, jump with both feet together, then three steps to the left.'

Schools can put textured strips on corridors or classroom equipment to guide pupils in the right direction.

Environmental awareness

Visually impaired children must be helped to become aware of their surroundings and learn how to cope with a range of situations both inside and outside. Walking them around the school enables them to touch walls, follow guidance strips, and learn the location of hazards and of necessary resources, such as the toilet roll in the toilet cubicle.

Games and leisure

It is sometimes difficult for children with sight problems to join in with informal games and conversations. You may be able to help here, by opening up possibilities for the child you work with to join in and become part of the group.

Social skills

The child with a visual impairment has a social communication problem as he or she cannot always see and therefore interpret the intentions of others. A major way in which children learn is through copying other children and adults, but a child with a visual impairment may be unable to see a great many actions, facial expressions and non-verbal messages and, as a result, will miss out on this type of learning. Do not be offended if these children use the wrong non-verbal messages and be prepared to teach them the acceptable ways of interacting in a group situation (e.g. remind the child to turn his or her face towards you when speaking). Some playground supervision may be necessary and your role might be to encourage inclusion of the child in group activities as far as possible.

Learning

Visually impaired children often miss out on ideas and meanings because of limited vision. It is therefore important to use 'hands on' experience whenever possible, e.g. when talking about leaves, give the child some leaves to hold or, better still, take the child to a park and let him or her feel a tree and walk through fallen leaves to hear the noise that makes.

Reading

There are a range of reading approaches necessary for children with visual impairment in terms of what is used (Braille, large print or Moon) and for this both resources and training are required:

- training for those teaching literacy to children in Braille and print (there is a considerable difference between knowing how to read Braille and knowing how to teach literacy through Braille)
- reading schemes used in schools, adapted for Braille and large print readers
- appropriate materials to read both for leisure and for National Curriculum studies

- access technology in schools to cater for a wide range of different visual needs
- training for pupils and teaching assistants as well as teachers in the applications of technology
- access to reading at home both for pleasure and homework purposes
- support for parents to help their children into literacy
- provision of appropriate materials for national tests and assessments, including GCSE
- textbooks and resource materials available in electronic format, with copyright issues resolved.

For children who read Braille or large print, it must be remembered that their speed of reading, and thus of information processing, is slower than that of fully sighted pupils. Visually impaired pupils cannot quickly scan a line or a page of text; they take longer than fully sighted pupils to explore and extract information from a graph, table or diagram and it takes longer for them to search a passage of text for the information to answer a question.

Where can more information be found?

- The LEA is likely to have specialist teachers or educational psychologists who can provide information and advice.
- Royal National Institute for the Blind, 224 Great Portland Street, London W1N 6AA www.rnib.org.uk
- The following resources are useful:
  A Blind Child in my Classroom (Gale and Cronin 1990).
  Spotlight on Special Educational Needs: Visual Impairment (Mason 2001).

Hearing impairment (HI)

There is a wide range of hearing impairment from mild to profound, although total lack of hearing is extremely rare. Recent statistics published by the National Deaf Children's Society estimated that there are about 25,000 deaf children with mild/moderate/profound hearing loss in our schools: 67 per cent are in mainstream schools, 14 per cent are in units in mainstream schools and 19 per cent are in special schools. These are pupils known to medical and educational support services. Approximately 800 children are born permanently deaf each year in the UK and every year a further million children experience temporary deafness caused by 'glue ear'. More pupils are being educated in mainstream schools than in the past. They have the support of peripatetic teachers with specialist knowledge but rely largely on the skills of teachers and assistants in schools.

What is hearing impairment?

There are different types and degrees of hearing loss:

Conductive hearing loss – This means any cause or condition which affects the progress of sound into the ear canal or across the middle ear. Conductive problems are often able to be treated by medicine or by surgery, e.g. glue ear, which occurs when fluid builds up in the middle ear and can be treated by an operation to insert a grommet. A significant number of young children suffer from glue ear and it can affect their language development.

Sensori-neural hearing loss – this means defects in the fine structure of the inner ear or sound pathways to the brain. Usually the high frequency sounds are most affected. This hearing loss is more likely to be permanent.

Mixed loss – when the child has both types of hearing loss. It is not enough to know that a child has a hearing loss; you need to know which sounds are affected and by how much.

Hearing losses are often described as ranging from slight to profound and are measured in decibels (dB):

Mild deafness – outside the normal range (greater than 21dB and less than 40 dB) – this would mean a child having difficulties in hearing faint or distant speech, difficulties listening in a classroom, difficulties in concentrating, and some delay in speech and language skills. Would hear a baby crying or music from a stereo.

Moderate deafness – (41–70dB) – this means significant difficulties for most children with speech and language and generally needing the use of hearing aids. Would hear a dog barking or a telephone ringing but may be unable to hear a baby crying.

Severe deafness – (71–95dB) – means speech may not be understood without hearing aids or lip-reading. Speech and language is severely affected. Would be able to hear a chainsaw or drums but not a piano or a barking dog.

Profound loss – (95dB and over) – means no speech is heard without hearing aids. Would be able to hear an aeroplane close by.

If a child is born deaf, or acquires hearing loss before learning to talk, their speech is severely affected. If a child goes deaf after learning to talk, their ability to talk is not lost. However, their speech may be impaired because of the child's inability to hear their own speech. The earlier a hearing loss is recognised, the sooner its effect can be reduced by treatment or by using hearing aids. Children who have a severe or profound loss do benefit from hearing aids, and some benefit from cochlear implants – electronic devices which bypass the damaged inner ear to stimulate the auditory nerve directly.

What are the learning implications?

Children who have normal hearing skills acquire ideas and concepts about the world around them largely through spoken language. The words we use to describe objects and experiences provide the child with a 'framework' to build on in order to learn effectively through reasoning and memory skills. For the child with a hearing impairment, understanding of language is limited, so this 'framework' which is vital for learning is incomplete. These children may then appear slow to learn, particularly in language-based tasks of speaking, listening, reading and writing. Reasoning and memory skills may also appear to be poor. However, many of these pupils have normal ability and good non-verbal and visual skills and most acquire spoken language in the same way as hearing children but at a slower rate. There are many factors which influence whether a hearing impaired child hears and understands speech. These include

- the kind and degree of hearing loss
- the age at which deafness developed
- the age at which it was discovered
- the issue and proper use of a suitable hearing aid
- early training
- the attentiveness of the child.

As a teaching assistant working with the child, you will find it helpful to be clear about these factors in the child's background in order to understand the hearing loss and its educational implications. Ask the specialist teacher of the hearing impaired to discuss this with you.

If you support a child with a hearing impairment you need to appreciate that the child has a *communication* problem and that your first task is to ensure as far as possible that the child is reliably receiving and understanding all communication from staff and pupils and is routinely participating in all class activities. Your role with the child who has a moderate to profound loss might involve ensuring the correct use of any hearing aid equipment provided for the child, and you may also need to learn a signing system if that is advised as appropriate for the child.

British Sign Language

British Sign Language (BSL) has recently (2003) been recognised by the government as an official minority language. It is used by about 70,000 people in the UK as their primary means of communication. It is the main means of communication for many deaf children in school and, as an assistant, you may need to attend classes in order to learn this language. 130,000 teaching assistants learn and use BSL to support deaf people. It can be used on its own or supported by the spoken word to enable lip-reading.

When working with a child with hearing impairment, please remember:
- Ensure the pupil is sitting in a position where they can see the teacher clearly and hear as much as possible. They will need to be close to the teacher to lip-read effectively.
- The pupil will find it difficult to know where sound is coming from and a lot of background noise will make things worse.
- Make eye contact and get the full attention of the child before speaking. He/she will need to look at you before any communication takes place.
- Rephrase, reiterate and extend your language whenever possible to give the child a better understanding of difficult concepts. Be creative!
- Reinforce as much spoken language as possible through the other senses.

Use visual aids and real experiences whenever you can. Visual clues through lip-reading, signing or natural gesture may be needed to ensure that the child understands. You may need to develop lively gestures and good facial expressions. You can be advised about this by a teacher of the hearing impaired.

- Do not assume that the child has understood the task they have to do. Check this by asking the child. Be patient!
- Pupils with moderate to profound hearing loss may be unable to acquire the skills of speaking, listening, reading and writing at a normal rate. (Most deaf children leave mainstream school at the age of 16 years with reading ages of about 9 years.) For such children it is essential to provide individual programmes to focus on the development of these skills. Appropriate activities and/or modifications to the curriculum may be advised by a specialist teacher, who will discuss your role in implementing them with you and the class teacher.
- Certain aids and technological supports are needed for the pupil to get maximum access to the curriculum. Hearing aids and radio systems are the child's link with the sounds around him/her. Learn how the systems work and how to monitor the development of listening skills.
- Communicating with others is a basic need. Pupils with hearing impairment may feel frustrated about their inability to communicate and so may lack self-esteem and occasionally become aggressive. You will need to establish communication with the child yourself and help others to do so. Be aware of social isolation and try to foster friendships and inclusion of the child within the peer group. You may also need to be particularly sensitive to the child's emotional needs. It has been estimated that 40–50 per cent of children who are deaf have emotional and behavioural difficulties to some degree, compared with 25 per cent in the rest of the population.
- Give plenty of encouragement!

For further advice

- The LEA is likely to have specialist teachers and educational psychologists who provide information or advice.
- The National Deaf Children's Society, 15 Dufferin Street, London EC1Y 8PD www.ndcs.org.uk
- Parents.

The following resources are useful:
Understanding Childhood Deafness (Quinn 1996)
Spotlight on Special Educational Needs – Hearing Impairment (Watson 2002).

Supporting pupils with physical disabilities

The term physical disability (PD) covers a wide range of conditions. The more common ones you are likely to come across include:

- cerebral palsy
- spina bifida
- hydrocephalus
- cystic fibrosis
- muscular dystrophy
- diabetes

- epilepsy
- haemophilia
- limb deficiency
- asthma
- brittle bone disease
- eczema

Within each category, the effects of the disability range from the relatively minor, such that the child can lead a 'normal' independent life, to relatively severe, such that the child cannot function without the support of caring adults.

There are many different physical impairments which may affect children and young people. There are several sources of information which will enable you to find out more. The Internet can be very helpful, particularly for some of the less common impairments. Some are very rare indeed and will need specialist medical support. In some cases, children with normal physical abilities lose some functions through disease or through traumatic injury.

Some pupils have relatively mild difficulties in coordination, fine motor skills (e.g. hand–eye coordination) or gross motor skills (e.g. coordination of arms and legs). This often results in dyspraxic difficulties which are discussed in Chapter 7. In this chapter we will consider your role in supporting children and young people who have physical disabilities.

Until quite recently, pupils with physical disabilities attended special schools, but ideas about physical disabilities have changed from the rather negative concept of 'handicap' to the more positive concepts of 'disability' or 'impairment'.

The right of people with disabilities to have access to normal experience has been recognised and the general public have become much more aware of people with disabilities and the part they play in community life. Now, whenever possible, these pupils should have their needs met in mainstream schools. There are still a considerable number of children whose additional needs are such that special schooling is appropriate at present. These are the pupils whose health is often at risk, who require very specialised equipment,

They wouldn't give us these labels if they had to wear them afterwards

or who require daily intensive physiotherapy, i.e. those who would 'fail to thrive' in a mainstream setting either physically or emotionally. In future more of these children will be educated in their local mainstream schools with the resources there to support them. As from 2003 all schools have to have an access plan.

Different disabilities result in different learning support needs. You will need to ask the teacher you work with about the details of the disability; educational psychologists, teacher advisers and school medical officers (doctors) can also give you details of associated learning difficulties and physical needs. For instance, pupils who have cerebral palsy sometimes have visuo-perceptual difficulties, i.e. they do not perceive visual images in the same way as other children; pupils with hydrocephalus sometimes have mood swings and times when they feel very tired; pupils with spina bifida sometimes have poor fine motor control (e.g. poor control of pencil and hand movements).

On the other hand, it is likely that pupils with medical needs alone, e.g. cystic fibrosis, epilepsy, asthma, brittle bone disease, will have no learning difficulties as such but they may need a sensitivity to other needs, e.g. tiredness, mood swings, and assistance in managing equipment or physiotherapy routines. These medical needs are explained in Chapter 12.

What is my role in giving support?

One step behind

Promoting independence is an essential part of your role with all pupils who need learning support. It is particularly important for pupils who have physical disabilities. You need to be 'one step behind' rather than 'one step ahead'. This means allowing the pupil to take calculated risks, on occasion – you will need to discuss this with the class teacher, head teacher, teacher adviser and sometimes the school medical officer, and think through the possible consequences!

It is a difficult task to maintain the balance between giving support and promoting independence. This involves you being clear about your expectations and firm in your directions without pressuring the child. However, sensitivity should tell you if and when to intervene.

Self-help

Part of your role may be enabling the child to look after himself or herself and to master those skills which able-bodied children take for granted, e.g. feeding, dressing, going to the toilet. When helping children in these ways it is important to treat them with dignity and respect and to provide privacy when appropriate.

Mobility

Pupils may need aids in the form of wheelchairs, crutches, mechanical limbs or callipers in order to get around. You will need to familiarise yourself with this equipment and make sure the pupil can use it with comfort and control. Most children learn to transfer themselves from place to place when required, e.g. from a wheelchair to the toilet, with little help. Younger children or very disabled pupils may need more help. If you need to assist in moving a child, you must know the correct techniques for lifting in order to avoid injury to either yourself or the child. Ask for support – quite literally! Lifting techniques must be taught, for each child, by the physiotherapist.

When working with a child with a physical disability, please remember:

- Behave towards him or her as you would to any other pupil of the same age.
- Do not do all the talking for the child or answer for him or her. Let the child make choices so he or she feels they have some control of their environment rather than becoming a passive recipient of support. Give him or her the *time* to make a response – these children often take longer to respond. Often their thinking response is immediate but controlling arms and legs, voice or equipment to aid communication can take time.
- Make sure you know the implications of the disability (physical, educational and emotional).
- Pupils with physical disabilities often become more tired than their classmates. Do recognise when they might need a break.

Cerebral palsy

The most common form of physical disability which has considerable learning implications is cerebral palsy.

What is cerebral palsy?

Cerebral palsy is not just one condition but a group of complicated conditions affecting movement and posture due to damage or failure in the development of the part of the brain which controls movement. The condition itself does not normally change, but people with it can, as they get older, become increasingly better at managing their difficulties.

Many forms of cerebral palsy are now recognised. It is often described either according to the *part* of the body affected:

- **Hemiplegia:** one side of the body
- **Diplegia:** upper limbs or lower limbs
- **Quadriplegia:** whole body affected.

or according to the *way* in which the body is affected:

- **Spasticity:** the person finds it very difficult to move their limbs so they have problems with posture and general movements.
- **Athetosis:** involuntary movements such as twitches or spasms.
- **Ataxia:** the person finds it difficult to coordinate their muscle groups so they have problems with balance, walking, etc.

It is sometimes the case that children have a mixture of these conditions, and other associated difficulties.

What are the learning implications?

There is a huge variation between individual children. The disability can be anything from a fairly minor condition, which affects the pupil's life only to a small extent, to a major disability affecting both the pupil's own life and that of his or her family.

It is important to realise that some (but not all) pupils who have cerebral palsy also have other difficulties with learning, e.g.

- perceptual difficulties
- communication difficulties
- movement and control difficulties
- difficulty in mixing socially – because it is hard to communicate
- visual difficulties.

The following helpful information comes from the website for SCOPE – a charity which supports people with cerebral palsy (www.scope.org.uk).

Visual function in children with cerebral palsy

If the child has a visual or spatial impairment, you may come across the following terms:

Acuity – How clearly he/she sees. Visual acuity is the first thing to check if the pupil appears to be having any difficulties with written or graphic materials. In one study of dyspraxic children, two thirds had normal visual acuity, but over two thirds had recognisable visual processing difficulties.

Motility – How well the child controls his/her eyes. Muscles control the eyes and these have to perform accurately in order for the child to be able to fix his or her gaze, move the eyes from left to right and find a word or picture on a page. If pupils have problems with motility they may not be able to copy work accurately or with any pace, particularly from the blackboard. Ask for optical checks to ensure that both eyes function together with a coordinated movement.

Constancy – Always seeing the shape in the same way. For some children the shape and size of the image they are looking at changes as they move their head or as each eye takes its turn at giving a picture. Experimenting with size and font against different coloured backgrounds can help.

Distractibility – Some children cannot screen out movement or light flickers. They may startle, lose concentration or even become aggressive. This interference may disrupt thought patterns and responses.

Figure ground – Whether the child can see one shape when it is embedded in other shapes.

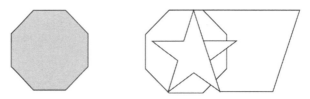

This is really important for retrieving written or graphic information from a crowded page or from the board.

Orientation – Can the child see the sameness of a shape if seen from a different angle?

This is important for mathematics and reading.

Memory – Can the child remember the shape if it is covered or removed? Kim's Game for younger children or the conveyor belt for older students can help them build this skill.

Depth perception – Can the child see the shape in three dimensions? If the child does not see well in three dimensions, he or she may not understand that a line drawing represents a solid object. In the worst cases the child may need to use cognitive skills to support a tactile picture of the solid object and know that it is solid even when seen as two-dimensional. Opticians have a simple test for depth perception.

Sequencing – Does the child appreciate the order that shapes are presented in? Children with poor ocular motility, constancy or memory may not organise their visual messages in sequence. This has an effect on reading and number work. Can the child build a memory of objects in sequence?

Closure – Filling in the bits of the picture that are not shown.

Remember that children with visual difficulties cannot tell you what they do not see and may not have the vocabulary to describe what they do see. Observation and testing in different conditions may give you a lead.

Communication

Because some children with cerebral palsy have little or no speech or writing, it is really important to identify ways in which they will be able to communicate. This may be through eye-pointing, where the assistant will need to recognise what the child is looking at.

There are now many computer-aided and touch-sensitive technologies which enable children to communicate. You may need to learn how these aids work and how the pupil might use them for communicating their needs.

It is very important to look for every possible way to communicate – but it is also important to keep a balance between accepting a pupil's genuine limitations and making sure they are provided with as many opportunities as possible to progress as far as they can.

The new computer technologies now developing are able to make significant differences to the quality of life of pupils with cerebral palsy.

How might the assistant give support?

- Encourage independence
- Help with moving the pupil from lesson to lesson; for example, removing obstacles
- Encourage support for the pupil from classmates
- Be clear about what equipment is needed and how to use it (the occupational therapist can advise)
- Enable communication
- Assist with toileting (in some circumstances), respecting the needs of the pupil
- Deliver a physiotherapy programme, under the guidance of a physiotherapist.

Other sources of information

- The LEA is likely to have specialist teachers or educational psychologists who can provide information or advice.
- SCOPE, 6–10 Market Road, London N7 0PW www.scope.org.uk
- Parents.

Spina bifida and hydrocephalus

Spina bifida is a congenital condition in which the spinal cord is partly exposed. Many children with spina bifida also have hydrocephalus. Hydrocephalus means that there is an abnormal amount of fluid in the brain. Most children will have a shunt (drain) surgically fitted which allows excess fluid to drain away from the brain. Eye defects are commonly associated with hydrocephalus. It can be life threatening if the shunt becomes blocked.

Symptoms indicating a blocked shunt include

- raised temperature
- headache
- drowsiness
- vomiting.

The pupil's health care plan will indicate the appropriate action but if you have any concerns you should consult the SENCO to obtain medical advice.

Children with spina bifida will need support with physical mobility and access to the curriculum. Pupils with hydrocephalus may have some learning difficulties (but not always) and will need support in following instructions and breaking down tasks into manageable steps.

Further useful information about supporting children with physical disabilities can be found in a booklet entitled *Working Together Towards Independence* (Fenton 1992).

12 Supporting pupils with medical needs

Most pupils will at some time in their school career have some medical needs. For the majority of children this usually amounts to minor first aid treatment for cuts and bruises or finishing a course of prescribed medication. For some pupils, the medical needs are long-term and require proper management both at home and in school. It is this group of pupils that we refer to as having medical needs.

Schools have been given guidance (DfEE 1996) to draw up policies to ensure that there are systems in place to manage the pupils' needs so that the impact of their medical condition does not adversely affect their progress, where at all possible. Schools will usually draw up an individual health care plan which details any safety measures that may be required to support a pupil with medical needs and to ensure other pupils are not put at risk.

As an assistant you may have a central role to play in the implementation of a pupil's health care plan. You may also be involved in supporting pupils with short-term medical needs or in giving minor first aid. It is important for you to be aware that your employer, usually the school or the LEA, has procedures for supporting pupils with medical needs, administering first aid and medication, and you need to be familiar with the procedures.

If you are asked to support pupils with medical needs, it is your employer's responsibility to make sure that as an employee you have full insurance cover for these duties. If you are asked to carry out any duties which you do not feel you are qualified or able to do you must ask your employer to provide you with appropriate training. This is particularly important with regard to lifting and handling of pupils and administering first aid and/or medication. In some cases pupils may have a potentially life-threatening medical condition and it is very important you have training in understanding the nature of the condition, what circumstances may pose a risk to the pupil and when the pupil may need extra support and attention. You will also need to be aware of the circumstances in which an emergency may arise and what action you should take in the event of an emergency. You will also need to be familiar with the back-up procedures in the event of a member of staff being absent.

Administering medication

If you agree to give medication or to supervise a pupil taking medication, you must have the appropriate training and guidance. In many cases the training will be provided by the staff of the school health service. Your school should have a clear policy which you are familiar with about the administration of prescribed and non-prescribed medication.

If you are in any doubt about any aspect of administering medication you should seek advice from the appropriate member of staff. Administration of any medication to a pupil under 16 years *always* requires the written consent of his/her parents/carers.

Before giving medication following the school policy you must check

- the pupil's name
- the written instructions from the parents or doctor for administering the medication
- the expiry date
- the dose prescribed.

It is always good practice to record every time medication is given and to sign and date the record.

Pupils with medical needs should be encouraged wherever possible to participate in all aspects of school life. As an assistant you may be asked to supervise and accompany a pupil who requires the administration of medication on a school trip. You must seek appropriate advice from your SENCO who will consult with the parents and seek further medical advice where necessary when the trip is being planned.

In schools there will be clear policies concerning the safe storage of medication. Pupils who use inhalers may need access to them at any time and you will need to know the procedure for their storage and to ensure accessibility of inhalers when required. You will also need to encourage older pupils to plan and manage the administration of their medication; for example, to ensure he/she takes his/her inhaler out onto the sports field during a games lesson so that it is immediately available.

Medical problems

Allergic reactions

Pupils can be allergic to a wide variety of substances and materials. The strength of the reaction can range from mild to severe. Symptoms can include

- swelling of the face, throat, tongue, lips
- difficulty in swallowing
- skin rash / flushed complexion
- raised heart rate
- stomach cramps and nausea
- difficulty in breathing / wheezing
- collapse / loss of consciousness.

The pupil's health care plan should indicate the reaction to known specific allergies and the appropriate actions. If there are any concerns about the severity of the reaction or the pupil does not respond to the prescribed medication, emergency hospital treatment should be sought.

Anaphylaxis

Anaphylaxis is an extreme allergic reaction which requires urgent medical treatment. The reaction can be caused by food, in particular nuts and dairy foods, or by wasp and bee stings. Where a pupil is at risk of a severe reaction he/she will usually be prescribed a pen-like device to administer a pre-measured dose of adrenalin. The use of such devices requires specific medical training, from a medical professional. The pupil's health care plan should give clear instructions as to the circumstances in which prompt emergency action will need to be taken.

Asthma

Asthma is very common. It is estimated that about one in seven children are diagnosed with it. Asthma causes the airways to narrow making it difficult to breathe. It can be triggered by a range of factors – cold air, dust mites, pollen, stress, exercise, etc. An asthma attack may include coughing, wheezing, difficulty in breathing out. Most pupils with asthma will use an inhaler (puffer) to relieve the symptoms. Some younger pupils may need to use a spacer device or a nebulizer to deliver their medication, which may require support from an adult. Pupils will need to be encouraged to take responsibility for taking their inhaler out onto the games field during outdoor games. It is important that asthmatic pupils have access to their inhaler at all times.

If a pupil has an attack you should

- encourage the pupil to use his/her inhaler
- sit them down and reassure them
- encourage them to breathe slowly.

If the prescribed medication does not take effect within five to ten minutes or the pupil becomes more distressed medical advice should be sought.

Cystic fibrosis

Cystic fibrosis is an inherited condition in which a sticky mucus is produced which affects the lungs in particular. The pancreas does not function properly in the digestion process.

The condition is usually controlled through daily physiotherapy, appropiate diet and the use of antibiotics. Children with cystic fibrosis often have a persistent cough. During a severe attack the pupil may cough up mucus or vomit.

Pupils with cystic fibrosis are susceptible to chest infections and may not be able to attend school for substantial periods of time. So they may need extra help to catch up when they return to school.

Sometimes assistants may be asked to perform the daily physiotherapy for pupils. This should only be carried out after appropriate medical training has been given and in consultation with the parents.

Diabetes

About one in 700 school age children has diabetes (DfEE 1996). It is a condition in which the body fails to control the blood sugar levels. Treatment for most pupils with diabetes is through insulin injections, monitoring the blood sugar levels and eating appropriately at regular intervals.

Most pupils will not need injections to be given during the school day. They are taught to give their own injections so will need only supervision and privacy in school. Children with diabetes may have to check their blood sugar levels. Most children are able to do this independently but will need privacy.

Diabetic pupils need to eat regularly and may need to eat during lesson times or before a games lesson. Staff will need to be aware that, during games, PE or other strenuous activity, a pupil may need to eat some sugar (glucose tablets or sweets) or to have a sugary drink. If the blood sugar level drops too low the child may experience what is often called a 'hypo', a hypoglycaemic episode. The symptoms of a 'hypo' may include

- sweating
- being very pale
- becoming sleepy or drowsy
- shaking
- becoming irritable.

Different children may exhibit different symptoms of a hypo. These specific signs should be described in the health care plan. If a pupil has a hypo they should be given glucose tablets, a sugary drink or chocolate bar as soon as possible and then something like biscuits or a sandwich when he/she has recovered. If the pupil does not recover within 15 minutes an ambulance should be called.

Eczema

Eczema is an allergic condition which affects the skin and can cause intense irritation. This may affect the pupil's concentration in lessons. The constant itching may also stop pupils sleeping and therefore affect learning ability. In severe cases periods of hospital treatment may be necessary which means the pupil may need additional support to catch up when he/she returns to school.

Epilepsy

One person in 150 suffers from some form of epilepsy. It can occur at any age. Most children with epilepsy will attend their local mainstream school. Not all people with epilepsy have major seizures. The severity and frequency of seizures vary. Not all seizures cause a loss of consciousness. There are different types of seizure. Some seizures are so brief that the child may not be aware of them and those working alongside the child may just think it is lack of concentration or a lapse in attention. These are known as absence seizures. Other seizures known as generalised seizures involve loss of consciousness. In a tonic closure seizure the child may become rigid and fall to the ground. The child may become incontinent and turn a bluish colour. There may also be movements of the whole body. After a seizure, the child may be confused and some pupils may need to sleep. Most epileptic seizures are controlled by medication.

Pupils with epilepsy will require extra supervision during some activities, e.g. practical science lessons, cookery, swimming, outdoor activities. Any concerns about participation in outdoor activities, school trips, etc. will need to be discussed with the parents and appropriate medical advice sought.

What should you do if a seizure occurs?

Once a seizure has started it is important to remove any potentially dangerous objects. The pupil should not be moved, but if possible something soft should be placed under their head, such as a jumper or jacket. Ensure that the pupil's airway is open but do not attempt to put anything into the mouth. When the seizure stops place the pupil in the recovery position and stay with him/her until he/she recovers. You may need to call an ambulance if the seizure is more prolonged than usual and the pupil does not appear to be recovering in the normal way or within the expected time.

Muscular dystrophy

Muscular dystrophy refers to a group of degenerative diseases that may start in childhood or adolescence. There is a degeneration in the muscles, which progressively affects fine and gross motor movements. Some forms of muscular dystrophy are inherited and young people may only live until their mid-twenties. Pupils will need increasing levels of support as their condition deteriorates. They will need wheelchair access and support for hand control; for example, non-slip mats, adapted cutlery and individually adapted computer switches. Although a pupil's condition may be deteriorating it is essential to try to ensure that with support they can achieve as much as possible and be successful.

In some circumstances you will also need to be familiar with the LEA lifting and handling policy and to have received appropriate training. You will need to be confident and clear about risk factors for individual pupils, emergency procedures and back-up procedures in the event of staff absence. You may also want to find out more about the particular medical condition of a pupil whom you support. There are many websites on the Internet which can help you find out more about a particular medical condition. Some useful addresses can be found in Appendix 1.

As an assistant the key principles for supporting pupils with medical needs are to be very familiar with the health care plan for each individual, and to make sure you have received appropriate training to support the needs of the pupil and you feel confident and clear about your role. Do not be afraid to ask for additional training or access to medical advice. If you are concerned always seek advice from your SENCO.

Appendix 1: helpful organisations

AFASIC 50–52 Great Sutton Street, London EC1V 0DJ; Tel: 020 7490 9411; Fax: 020 7251 2834; email: info@afasic.org.uk website: www.afasic.org.uk

Association for Spina Bifida and Hydrocephalus Asbah House, 42 Park Road, Peterborough PE1 2UQ; Tel: 01733 555988; website: www.asbah.org

British Deaf Association 1–3 Worship Street, London EC2A 2AB; Tel: 020 7588 3520; website: www.britishdeafassociation.org.uk

British Diabetic Association UK 10 Parkway, Camden, London NW1 7AA; Tel: 020 7424 1000; Fax: 020 7424 1001; email: info@diabetes.org.uk website: www.diabetes.org.uk

British Dyslexia Association 98 London Road, Reading RG1 5AU; Tel: 0118 966 8271; Fax: 0118 935 1927; website: www.bda-dyslexia.org.uk

British Epilepsy Association New Anstey House, Gate Way Drive, Yeadon, Leeds LS19 7XY; Tel: 01132 108800; Helpline: 0808 8005050; website: www.epilepsy.org.uk

Cystic Fibrosis Trust 11 London Road, Bromley, Kent BR1 1BY; Tel: 020 8464 7211; website: www.cftrust.org.uk

Disability Rights Commission DRC Helpline, Freepost, MID 02164, Stratford-Upon-Avon, Warwickshire CV37 9BR; Tel: 08457 622 633; Fax: 08457 778 878; email: enquiry@drc-gb.org website: www.drc-gb.org

Down's Syndrome Association 155 Mitcham Road, London SW17 9PG; Tel: 020 8682 4001; email: info@downs-syndrome.org.uk website: www.downs-syndrome.org.uk

Dyspraxia Foundation 8 West Alley, Hitchin, Hertfordshire SG5 1EG; Tel: 01462 454986; website: www.dyspraxiafoundation.org.uk

Haemophilia Society Chesterfield House, 385 Euston Road, London NW1 3AU; Tel: 020 7380 0600; Fax: 020 7387 8220; email: infor@haemophilia.org.uk website: www.haemophilia.org.uk

LADDER (National Learning and Attention Deficit Disorders Association) 142 Mostyn Road, London SW19 3LR

MENCAP 117–123 Golden Lane, London EC1Y 0RT; Tel: 020 7454 0454;

Fax: 020 7696 5540; email: information@mencap.org.uk website: www.mencap.org.uk

National Association for Special Educational Needs (NASEN) 4–5 Amber Business Village, Amber Close, Amington, Tamworth, Staffs B77 4RP; Tel: 01827 311500; Fax: 01827 313 005; email: welcome@nasen.org.uk website: www.nasen.org.uk

National Asthma Campaign Providence House, Providence Place, London N1 0NT; Tel: 020 7226 2260; Helpline: 08457 010203; website: www.asthma.org.uk

National Autistic Society 393 City Road, London EC1V 1NG; Tel: 020 7833 2299; Fax: 020 7833 9666; email: nas@nas.org.uk website: www.nas.org.uk

National Blind Children's Society Bradbury House, Market Street, Highbridge, Somerset TA9 3BW; Tel: 01278 764 764; Fax: 01278 764 790; email: businessenquiries@nbcs.org.uk website: www.nbcs.org.uk

National Deaf Children's Society 15 Dufferin Street, London EC1Y 8UR; Tel: 0808 800 8880; Fax: 020 7251 5020; email: helpline@ndcs.org.uk website: www.ndcs.org.uk

National Eczema Society Hill House, Highgate Hill, London N19 5NA; Tel: 08702 413 604 / 020 7281 3553; Fax: 020 7281 6395; website: www.eczema.org

National Society for Epilepsy Chesham Lane, Chalfont St Peter, Buckinghamshire SL9 0RJ; Tel: 01494 601 300; Helpline: 01494 601 400; Fax: 01494 871 927; website: www.epilepsynse.org.uk

Royal National Institute for Deaf People (RNID) 19–23 Featherstone Street, London EC1Y 8SL; Tel: 020 7296 8000; Fax: 020 7296 8199; email: informationline@rnid.org.uk website: www.rnidp.org.uk

Royal National Institute for the Blind (RNIB) 105 Judd Street, London WC1H 9NE; Tel: 020 7388 1266; Fax: 020 7388 2034; website: www.rnib.org.uk

SCOPE 6–10 Market Road, London N7 0PW; Tel: 020 7619 7100; Helpline: 0808 800 3333; website: www.swpe.org.uk

Appendix 2: glossary

Asperger's Syndrome

Asperger's Syndrome is thought to be a form of autism. Many children with this problem will appear odd or peculiar to others: they may use a set form of language and set responses in a number of different social situations; they will have a limited number of friends; they will develop unusual interests which preoccupy them; they often appear clumsy and have difficulty in expressing themselves with facial expressions or gestures.

Asthma

Asthma is the most common chronic disease in childhood and can be described as a wheezing bronchitis causing the airways in the lungs to narrow, which makes it difficult for the child to breathe.

Attention deficit disorder (ADD)

Children with ADD are characterised by inattentiveness and impulsive behaviour. Typically, they cannot remain on task for more than a few minutes. They are easily distracted by external stimuli. Socially, they may appear naïve, lack inhibitions or behave inappropriately. ADD may be accompanied by hyperactivity. Children with AD(H)D are also over-active, restless and fidgety. Some children with AD(H)D are on medication such as Ritalin.

Auditory perception

The identification and analysis of information through the ears. There are various elements including:

- *attention* – the ability to focus on or respond to sounds
- *discrimination* – the ability to distinguish between different sounds and noises
- *memory* – the ability to store auditory information in short-term memory
- *sequencing* – the ablity to recall information in the correct order.

Autism

Autism is a developmental disability characterised by a lack of interaction and communication with others. There are often obsessive behaviours and strong attachment to routine and order, and a lack of imagination. Many autistic children have severe learning difficulties.

Cerebral palsy

Children with cerebral palsy will have a number of abnormalities in movement and posture, as a result of damage to the brain. Head control is poor and speech is often affected.

Coeliac disease

Children with coeliac disease require a special gluten-free diet.

Cognitive

Relating to intellectual activity, the thinking or knowing part of an activity rather than feeling.

Comprehension

The understanding of what is said or what is read.

Concept

An idea that can be abstract or concrete. Concepts are usually learned through experience or activities and then a verbal label is learned by association, e.g. a young child learns the concept of cold by experiencing coldness in ice cream, the fridge, ice cubes, metal objects, etc.

Coordination

The combination of several actions or functions to perform a task:

- gross motor coordination refers to the coordination of muscle activities to perform big movements, e.g. running, walking, sitting
- fine motor coordination refers to the coordination of small muscle movements to perform precise tasks, e.g. writing, using scissors, picking up small objects
- hand–eye coordination (also known as visual-motor coordination) is the ability to coordinate visual activities and muscle movements to complete an activity such as hitting a tennis ball with a racquet.

Correspondence

Matching two separate bits of information, e.g. grapheme–phoneme correspondence is to match letter shapes with the speech sound.

Cystic fibrosis

A hereditary disease which produces a thick and sticky mucus on the lungs and pancreas. This can block the airways and lead to infection.

Decode

To convert a written or spoken code into meaningful language.

Diabetes

Children with diabetes have too much blood sugar (glucose) and are unable to convert it into energy because they do not have enough insulin.

Discrimination

The ability to perceive differences between two or more stimuli.

Down's Syndrome

Children with Down's Syndrome will have distinct physical characteristics. Most will have moderate to severe learning difficulties with varying degrees of sensory impairment.

Dyslexia

This is a specific learning difficulty affecting the ability to read and/or spell. Now thought to be a genetic neuronal deficiency often affecting auditory memory.

Dyspraxia

Dyspraxia is an impairment or immaturity of the organisation of movement. Children with dyspraxia will have poor coordination, poor perception (e.g. problems with following directions), poor handwriting, and show problems with self-help skills (e.g. dressing, tying shoelaces).

Eczema

Eczema appears as a red scaly rash behind the ears, on the cheeks, in the folds of the elbows, behind the knees, or on the hands and wrists.

Epilepsy

Children with epilepsy have recurrent seizures ranging from mild (absence seizures) to severe seizures, which may be clonic (rapid muscular contractions and relaxations) or tonic (prolonged uniform muscular spasm).

Hydrocephalus

Children with hydrocephalus have an abnormal amount of fluid in the brain.

Kinaesthesis

A sensation of the body's movement or of musculer effort.

Metacognition

An understanding of the learning process and how it develops.

Mnemonic

A strategy used to help memorise information in the correct sequence; e.g. in spelling, the construction of a sentence with the initial letter of each word matching the sequence of letters in the word to be learned.

Motor movement

- *Fine motor* – activities involving small areas of the musculature of the body
- *Gross motor* – activities involving large areas of the musculature of the body and particularly the large muscle groups, e.g. skipping
- *Motor-perceptual* – this describes the linkage between the child's brain and their body's capacity to respond physically to the environment.

Multi-disciplinary

Involving several different disciplines, often professions, in the resolution of problems.

Multi-sensory

Using all the sensory pathways: tactile, visual, auditory, etc.

Paired reading

A way of sharing a book with a child in which the adult and child read aloud together.

Perseveration

A tendency to continue repeating sounds, symbols or activities inappropriately immediately after relevant usage in speech or in writing.

Phoneme

The smallest unit of sound in a language; it may be represented by one or more letters.

Phonics

A strategy for decoding words by linking sounds (phonemes) to letter symbols (graphemes).

Phonological awareness

Awareness of sounds and being able to recognise and manipulate sounds.

Plenary

The plenary comes at the end of a literacy hour or a maths lesson. It is the time for the teacher to review the teaching targets of the lesson and to assess what the children have learned. It is also a time for the children to reflect on what they have done and how well they have achieved the targets.

Segment

To break words into their component phonemes, e.g. man: m–a–n, or into syllables, e.g. letter: let–ter.

Semantic cue

Information from adjoining words, phrases or sentences, used to help in the identification of an unfamiliar word.

Shared reading

A strategy in which the teacher models reading skills with a group of children.

Sight vocabulary

Words which a child can read automatically as whole words.

Spatial orientation

Awareness of how the body relates to the environment or how shapes and objects relate to each other in space.

Spina bifida

A failure of the bones enclosing the spinal cord to develop properly. Eighty per cent of children with spina bifida also have hydrocephalus.

Visual discrimination

The ability to perceive similarities and differences in visually presented material.

Visual memory

The ability to store visually presented information in order to analyse it and recall it accurately.

Visual perception

The organisation and interpretation of information received through the eyes.

Visual sequencing

The order in which visual information is presented.

Writing frame

Any structure that supports writing. It may consist of pictures, diagrams, headings or questions. It may be in the form of a template for a specific writing format.

Bibliography

Ainscow, M. (1998) 'Reading out to all learners', talk given at Bournemouth SENCO conference.

Ainscow, M. and Tweddle, D.A. (1988) *Encouraging Classroom Success.* London: David Fulton Publishers.

ATL (1998) *Achievement for All.* London: ATL.

Attwood, T. (1998) *Asperger's Syndrome: A Guide for Parents and Professionals.* London: Jessica Kingsley Publishers.

Audit Commission (1992) *Getting in on the Act: A Review of Progress in Special Educational Needs.* London: HMSO.

Bennett, A. (1985) 'Meeting the integration needs of partially hearing unit pupils'. *AEP Journal*, **6** (5), Supplement.

Bernstein, B. (1961) 'Social class and linguistic development: a theory of social learning', in A.H. Halsey, J. Floyd and C.A. Anderson (eds), *Education, Economy and Society.* New York: Free Press.

Blind and Partially Sighted Children in Britain. The RNIB Survey, Vol. 12. London: HMSO.

Cooper, P. and Ideus, K. (1995) *Attention Deficit (Hyperactivity) Disorder: Educational, Medical and Cultural Issues.* East Sutton: AWCEBD.

Cooper, P. and Ideus, K. (1996) *Attention Deficit/Hyperactivity Disorder: A Practical Guide for Teachers.* London: David Fulton Publishers.

Daines, B., Fleming, P. and Miller, C. (1996) *Spotlight on Special Educational Needs: Speech and Language Difficulties.* London: NASEN.

DfEE (1994) *Code of Practice on the Identification and Assessment of Special Educational Needs.* London: DfEE.

DfEE (1996) *Supporting Pupils with Medical Needs: A Good Practice Guide.* London: HMSO.

DfEE (1998a) *National Literacy Strategy: A Framework for Teaching Literacy.* London. DfEE.

DfEE (1998b) *Excellence for All*, Green Paper. London: HMSO.

DfEE (1999a) *The Management, Role and Training of Learning Support Assistants.* Centre for Educational Needs, University of Manchester. London: DfEE.

DfEE (1999b) *National Numeracy Strategy: A Framework for Teaching Mathematics.* London: DfEE.

DfEE/QCA (1998b) *Supporting the Target Setting Process*. London: DfEE.

DfES (2000) *Supporting Pupils with Special Educational Needs in the Literacy Hour*. London: DfES.

DfES (2001a) *Special Educational Needs Code of Practice*. London: DfES.

DfES (2001b) *SEN Toolkit*. London: DfES.

DfES (2001c) *National Numeracy Strategy Towards the National Curriculum for Mathematics: Examples of what Pupils with Special Educational Needs should be able to do at each P Level*. London: DfES.

DfES (2002) *National Literacy Strategy Towards the National Curriculum for English: Examples of what Pupils with Special Educational Needs should be able to do at each P Level*. London: DfES.

Disability Rights Commission (2002) *Code of Practice for Schools*. London: DRC.

Fenton, M. (1992) *Working Together Towards Independence*. London: RADAR – the Royal Association for Disability and Rehabilitation.

Fox, G. and Halliwell, M. (2000) *Supporting Literacy and Numeracy: A Guide for Learning Support Assistants*. London: David Fulton Publishers.

Gale, G. and Cronin, P. (1990) *A Blind Child in My Classroom*. London: RNIB.

Howlin, P., Baron-Cohen, S. and Hadwin, J. (1998) *Teaching Children with Autism to Mind Read*. Chichester: Wiley.

La Vigna, G. W. (1992) *Positive Approaches to Solving Behavior Challenges*. Los Angeles, Ca: Institute for Applied Behavioral Analysis.

Lock, A. (1985) *Living Language*. London: NFER.

Maines, B. and Robinson, G. (1988) 'A Bag of Tricks, Video workshop pack. Bristol: Lucky Duck Publications.

Maines, B. and Robinson, G. (1992) *You Can – You Know You Can. Course handbook to accompany workshops on the self-concept approach*. Bristol: Lucky Duck Publications.

Mason, H. (2001) *Spotlight on Special Educational Needs: Visual Impairment*. London: NASEN.

Porter, J. and Ashdown, R. (2002) *Pupils with Complex Learning Difficulties: Promoting Using Visual Materials and Methods*. London: NASEN.

QCA (2000) *Curriculum Guidance for the Foundation Stage*. London: HMSO.

QCA (2001) *Planning, Teaching and Assessing the Curriculum for Pupils with Learning Difficulties: A General Guide*. London: HMSO.

Quinn, W. R. (1996) *Understanding Childhood Deafness*. London: Harper Collins.

Ripley, K., Daines, B. and Barrett, J. (1997) *Dyspraxia: A Guide for Teachers and Parents*. London: David Fulton Publishers.

Sisson, E. (1994a) *Language Comes First*. Special Children Magazine. Questions Publications.

Sisson, E. J. (1994b) *A Simple Model to Explain Language Difficulties in Special Children*. Questions Publications.

Stobbs, P. and Rieser, R. (2002) *Making it Work: Removing Disability Discrimination – Are you Ready?* London: Council for Disabled Children and Disability Equality in Education.

Watson, L. (2002) *Spotlight on Special Educational Needs: Hearing Impairment*. London: NASEN.

Index